The Complete Book

B.C. Lester B

CONTEN

Hey! Thanks for buying this book, I hope you enjoy it. All feedback is welcomed. If you have any queries, suggestions or want to get in touch, then email me at ben@bclesterbooks.com. Are you a fan, or just interested in flags, maps and geography in general? Then join our community of people alike:

FACEBOOK: World Flags and Facts

INSTAGRAM: @worldflagsandfacts

Is this book misprinted? Email ben@bclesterbooks.com and we will send a replacement copy!

B.C. LESTER BOOKS

Who is B.C. Lester?

We are a small publishing firm based in Buckinghamshire, UK and we aim to make quality geography titles for the whole family. We have released several activity, trivia and fact books in geography, and are working hard to bring a wider selection for kids and adults, so if you have any title you would like to see, email ben@bclesterbooks.com. We are all ears. And if you want to be part of the family, follow our socials.

Books we think you will like

Can you work out all the countries from their outlines?

Country maps, facts, flags and coat of arms with their meanings.

Can you name the country the flag belongs to?

Titles coming soon

- Flag Coloring Book
- U.S. State Flags Coloring Book
- U.S. State Factbook
- Flags and Facts of the World for Kids
- World geography: The Big Book of Wordsearches
- World Geography: The Big Book of Crosswords
- World Geography: The Activity Book for Kids
- World Geography Trivia: The Ultimate Quiz Book
- Cityscapes coloring book
- 1000 Fun World Facts You Didn't Know Before

Want to stay in touch? Then visit go.bclesterbooks.com to find out about our next releases and help yourself to a freebie.

Notes on this Book

- Country stats include stats of areas that form the constituent entity of a country, e.g. Aruba and The Netherlands, but exclude self-governing entities e.g. Greenland and Denmark. This is true for measures of population, area, highest point and GDP.
- Kosovo is included in Serbia's statistics, although a later revision will likely see Kosovo listed as it's own independent country.
- Taiwan is currently not represented by any country, and it is not recognised as it's own country by the majority of UN member states.
- English names are given for all countries, although in a later revision, the countries of Ivory Coast, Cape Verde and East Timor will be edited respectively.

CREDITS

- Country map graphics created using MapChart.

OUR DEFINITION OF STATISTICS GIVEN

- **Capital City:** All capitals regardless of status are written here, separated by dashes. E.g. Bolivia's capitals would be La Paz / Sucre
- **Area**: The total area of a country, including it's land area and water area in km^2 and square miles in brackets.
- **Population:** Population of the country as of 2019.
- **Highest Point:** The highest point in altitude of land belonging to the country's constituent area.
- **Official Languages:** Languges with special status used by the government. National languages are languages used by the majority of the country, and are given in brackets when the official language is not specified.
- **GDP**: Nominal Gross Domestic Product of the country as of 2019.
- **Currency:** Official currency of use within a country.
- **Major Religions:** In the context of this book, major religions of a country are religions which over 25% of the population of a country adhere to.
- **Government:** The type of government. Defining the form and system of government.
- **Geography**: In the context of this book, geography are climatic zones found to any extent within the country. 'Mountain' is used to define an alpine climate.
- **Time Zone:** All time zones found within a country, separated by commas.
- **Major Cities:** In the context of this book, major cities are all cities with a large population (metro or other) relative to the size of other cities within the country.

Earth & Continents Facts

Earth

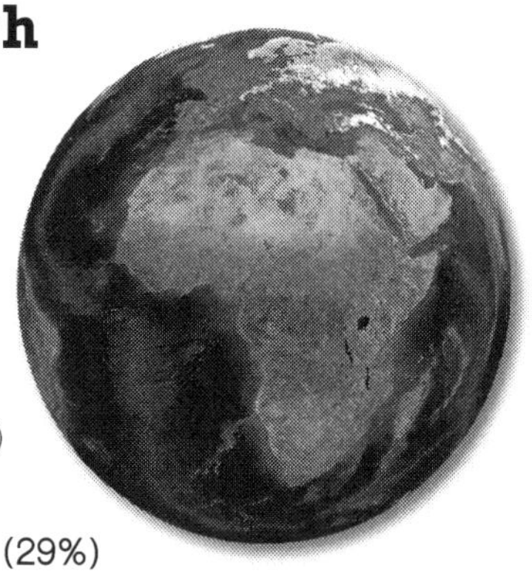

DIAMETER:

12,742km (7919 miles)

CIRCUMFERENCE:

40,075km (24,901 miles)

TOTAL SURFACE AREA:

510,000,000km^2 (196,940,000 sq mi)

LAND SURFACE AREA:

148,326,000km^2 (57,268,900 sq mi) **(29%)**

TOTAL WEIGHT:

5.972x10^{24} kg

WORLD BIOMES:

- Polar **8%**,
- Tundra **4%**,
- Taiga (Coniferous) **13%**,
- Temperate (Deciduous, Grassland) **18%**,
- Mediterranean **2%**,
- Desert (Shrubland, Arid) **32%**,
- Tropical (Savanna, Rainforest) **20%**,
- Mountain **3%**

EARTH RECORDS

HIGHEST MOUNTAIN: Mount Everest - 8848m (Nepal/China)

LONGEST RIVER: River Nile – 6650km (4133 miles) *(disputed)*

LARGEST ISLAND: Greenland – 2,160,000km^2 (836,330 sq miles)

LARGEST LAKE: Caspian Sea – 371,000km^2 (146,000 sq miles)

LARGEST CITY BY POPULATION: Tokyo-Yokohama – 38,000,000 people (Japan)

HIGHEST WATERFALL: Angel Falls – 979m (Venezuela)

DEEPEST OCEAN: Mariana Trench – 10,984m

HOTTEST TEMPERATURE RECORDED: 56.7°C/134.1°F – Furnace Creek, USA *(disputed)*

COLDEST TEMPERATURE RECORDED: -89.2°C/-128.6°F – Vostok Station, Antarctica

Continents Of The World

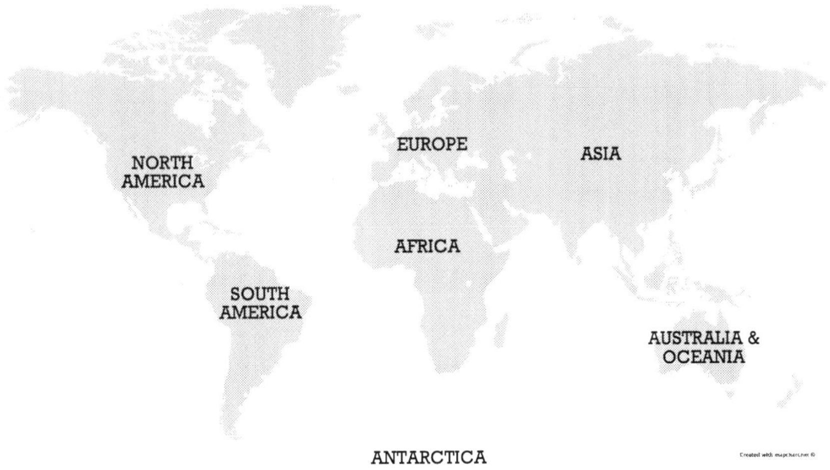

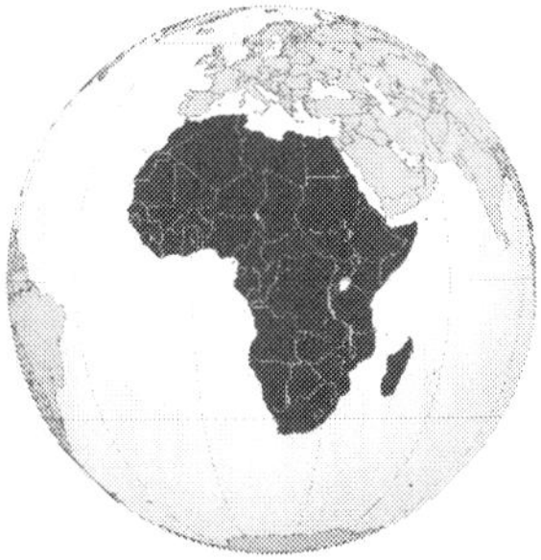

AFRICA

Area: 30,370,000km² (11,730,000 sq. miles)
Population: 1,200,000,000
Countries: 54
GDP: $2.45 trillion
Highest Point: Mt Kilimanjaro, Tanzania (5895m)
Largest City: Cairo, Egypt
Largest Country: Algeria
Longest River: River Nile 6650km (4130 mi)
Largest Lake: Lake Victoria
Largest Island: Madagascar
Tallest Waterfall: Mutarazi Falls (762m)

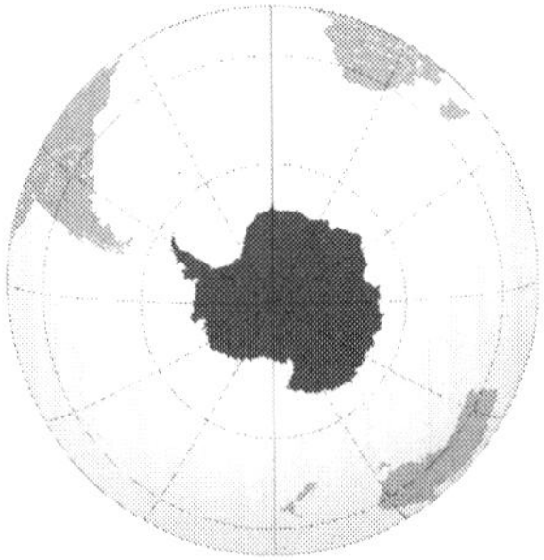

ANTARCTICA

Area: 14,000,000km² (5,400,000 sq. miles)
Population: 1106
Countries: 0
Highest Point: Vinson Massif (4892m)
Largest Lake: Vostok
Largest Island: Alexander Island

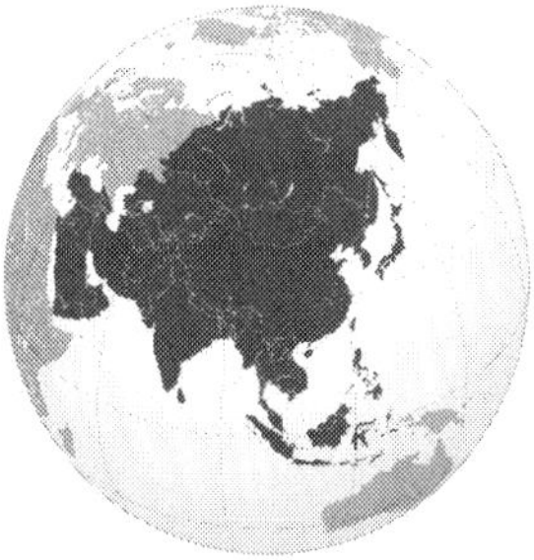

ASIA

Area: 44,579,000km² (17,212,000 sq. miles)
Population: 4,600,000,000
Countries: 49
GDP: $31.58 trillion
Highest Point: Mount Everest, Nepal/China (8848m)
Largest City: Tokyo, Japan
Largest Country: Russia
Longest River: Yangtze River, China
Largest Lake: Caspian Sea
Largest Island: Borneo
Tallest Waterfall: -

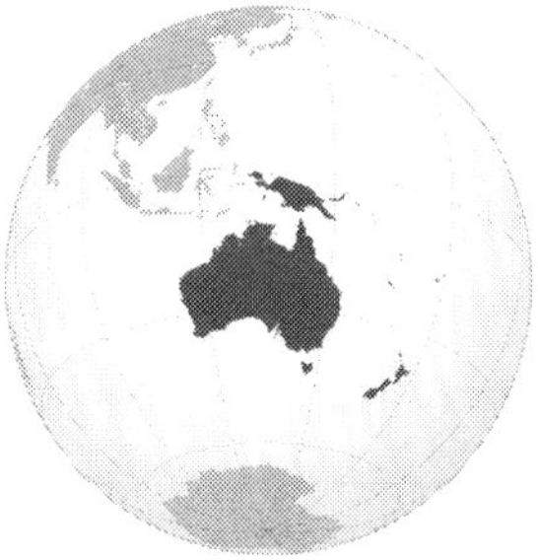

AUSTRALIA AND OCEANIA

Area: 8,525,989km² (3,291,903 sq. miles)
Population: 42,000,000
Countries: 15
GDP: $1.63 trillion
Highest Point: Puncak Jaya, Indonesia (4884m)
Largest City: Sydney, Australia
Largest Country: Australia
Longest River: River Murray, Australia
Largest Lake: -
Largest Island: New Guinea
Tallest Waterfall: Chamberlain Falls (700m)

EUROPE

Area: 10,180,000km² (3,930,000 sq. miles)
Population: 743,000,000
Countries: 50
GDP: $21.79 trillion
Highest Point: Mount Elbrus, Russia (5642m)
Largest City: Istanbul, Turkey
Largest Country: Russia
Longest River: River Danube
Largest Lake: Lake Lagoda
Largest Island: Great Britain
Tallest Waterfall: Vinnufossen (860m)

NORTH AMERICA

Area: 24,709,000km² (9,540,000 sq. miles)
Population: 579,024,000
Countries: 23
GDP: $24.43 trillion
Highest Point: Denali, USA (6198m)
Largest City: New York City, USA
Largest Country: Canada
Longest River: River Mississippi
Largest Lake: Lake Superior (82,100km²)
Largest Island: Greenland
Tallest Waterfall: Colonial Creek Falls (788m)

SOUTH AMERICA

Area: 17,850,000km² (6,890,000 sq. miles)
Population: 423,581,000
Countries: 13
GDP: $3.64 trillion
Highest Point: Aconcagua, Brazil (6962m)
Largest City: Sao Paulo, Brazil
Largest Country: Brazil
Longest River: Amazon River
Largest Lake: Titicaca
Largest Island: Isla Grande De Tierra Del Fuego
Tallest Waterfall: Angel Falls (979m)

A-Z Countries of the World

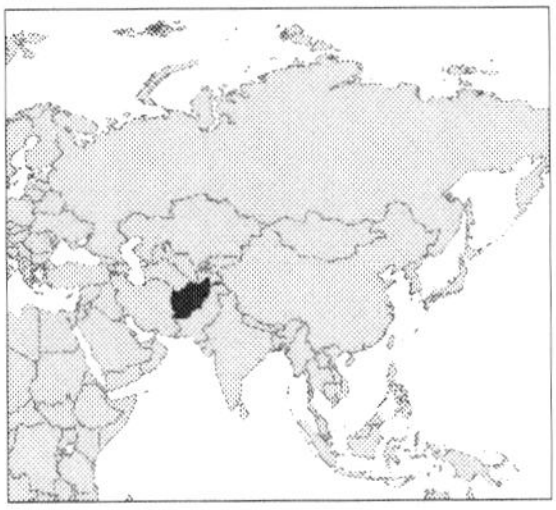

Afghanistan in Asia

AFGHANISTAN

Capital City: Kabul
Area: 652,230 km^2 (251,830 sq mi)
Population: 31,575,018
Highest Point: Noshaq (7492m)
Official Languages: Dari/Pashto
GDP: $21.54 billion
Currency: Afghani
Major Religions: Islam
Government: Unitary Presidential Islamic Republic
Geography: Mountain, Desert
Time Zone: UTC+4:30
Major Cities: Kabul, Kandahar, Herat

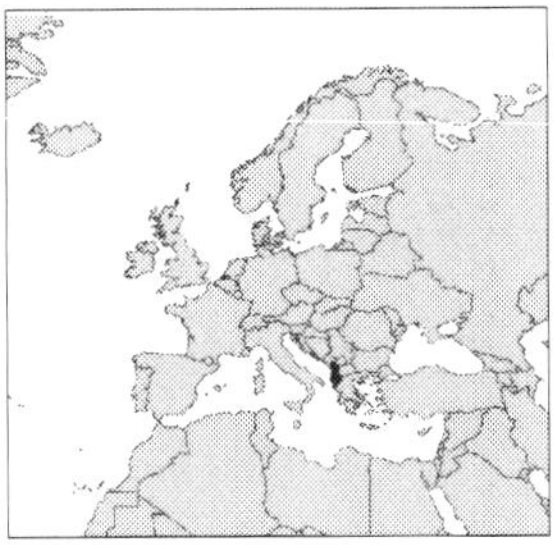

Albania in Europe

ALBANIA

Capital City: Tirana
Area: 28,748 km^2 (11,100 sq mi)
Population: 2,876,591
Highest Point: Mt. Korab (2764m)
Official Languages: Albanian
GDP: $15.12 billion
Currency: Lek
Major Religions: Islam
Government: Unitary Parliamentary Constitutional Republic
Geography: Mediterranean, Mountain, Temperate
Time Zone: UTC+1
Major Cities: Tirana, Durres

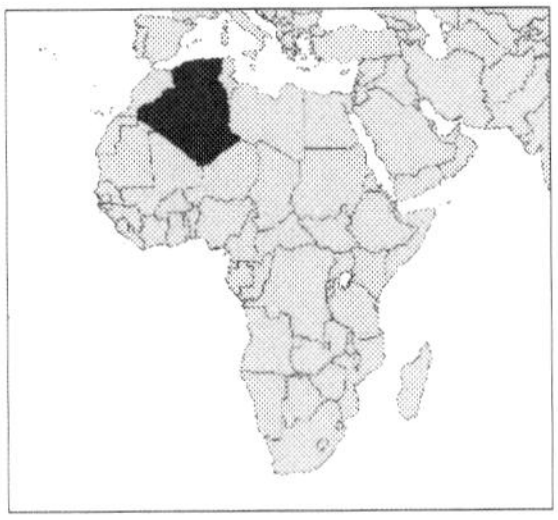

Algeria in Africa

ALGERIA

Capital City: Algiers
Area: 2,381,741 km^2 (919,595 sq mi)
Population: 42,200,000
Highest Point: Mt. Tahat (3003m)
Official Languages: Arabic/Berber
GDP: $180.69 billion
Currency: Dinar
Major Religions: Islam
Government: Unitary Semi-presidential Constitutional Republic
Geography: Mediterranean, Mountain, Desert
Time Zone: UTC+1
Major Cities: Algiers, Oran, Constantine

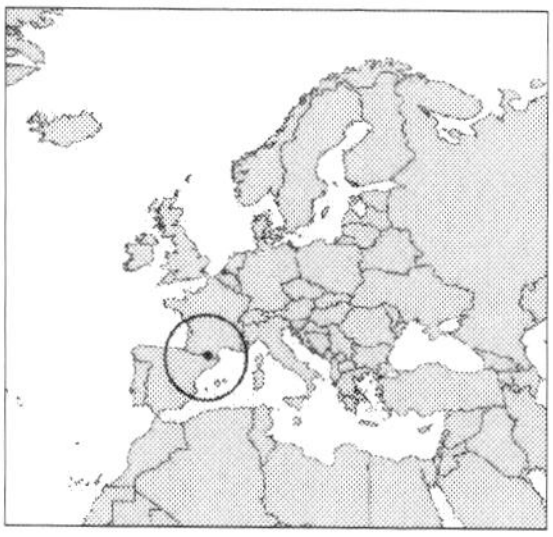

Andorra in Europe

ANDORRA

Capital City: Andorra La Vella
Area: 468 km² (181 sq mi)
Population: 77,281
Highest Point: Coma Pedrosa (2942m)
Official Languages: Catalan
GDP: $3.24 billion
Currency: Euro
Major Religions: Christianity
Government: Unitary Parliamentary Semi-elective diarchy
Geography: Mountain
Time Zone: UTC+1
Major Cities: Andorra La Vella

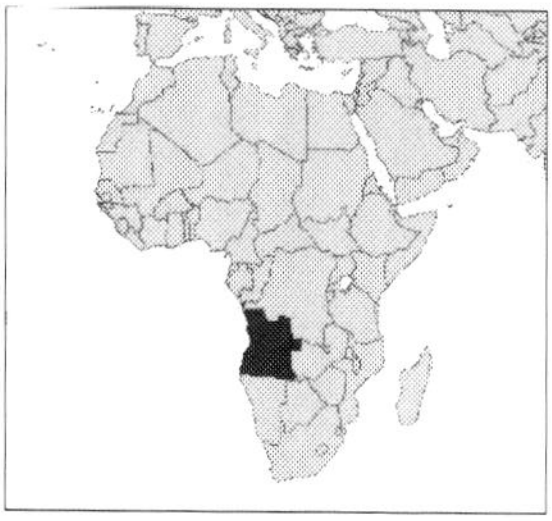

Angola in Africa

ANGOLA

Capital City: Luanda
Area: 1,246,700km² (481,400 sq mi)
Population: 25,789,024
Highest Point: Morro De Moco (2620m)
Official Languages: Portuguese
GDP: $124.60 billion
Currency: Kwanza
Major Religions: Christianity
Government: Unitary Presidential Constitutional Republic
Geography: Savannah, Mountain, Desert
Time Zone: UTC+1
Major Cities: Luanda, Lubango, Huambo, Benguela

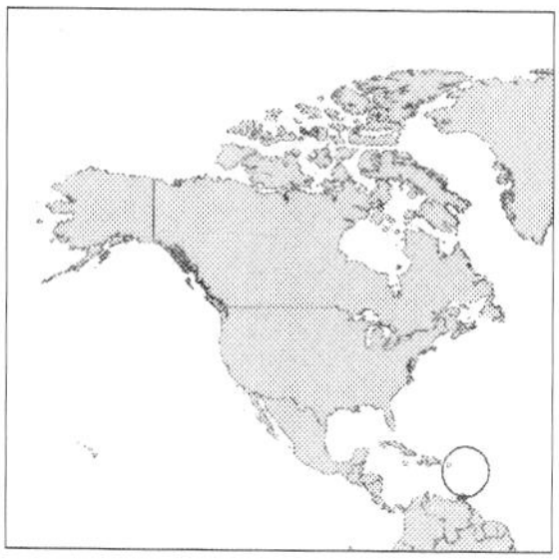

Antigua and Barbuda in North America

ANTIGUA AND BARBUDA

Capital City: St. Johns
Area: 440km² (170 sq mi)
Population: 100,963
Highest Point: Mt. Obama (402m)
Official Languages: English
GDP: $1.72 billion
Currency: East Caribbean Dollar
Major Religions: Christianity
Government: Unitary Parliamentary Constitutional Monarchy
Geography: Tropical
Time Zone: UTC-4
Major Cities: St. Johns

Argentina in South America

ARGENTINA

Capital City: Buenos Aires
Area: 2,780,400km² (1,073,500 sq mi)
Population: 43,847,430
Highest Point: Aconcagua (6962m)
Official Languages: (Spanish)
GDP: $445.47 billion
Currency: Peso
Major Religions: Christianity
Government: Federal Presidential Constitutional Republic
Geography: Mountain, Temperate, Desert
Time Zone: UTC-3
Major Cities: Buenos Aires, Cordoba, Rosario, Mendoza

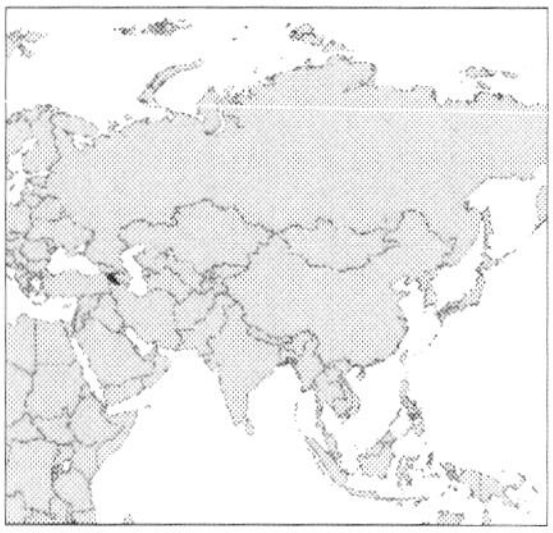

Armenia in Asia

ARMENIA

Capital City: Yerevan
Area: 29,743km² (11,484 sq mi)
Population: 2,924,816
Highest Point: Mt. Aragats (4049m)
Official Languages: Armenian
GDP: $13.30 billion
Currency: Dram
Major Religions: Christianity
Government: Unitary Parliamentary Republic
Geography: Mountain, Temperate
Time Zone: UTC+4
Major Cities: Yerevan, Gyumri, Vanadzor

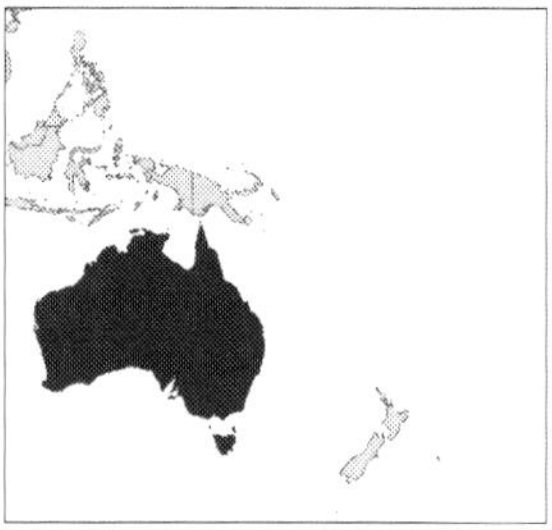

Australia in Australia and Oceania

AUSTRALIA

Capital City: Canberra
Area: 7,692,024 km² (2,969,907 sq mi)
Population: 25,330,200
Highest Point: Mt. Kosciuszko (2620m)
Official Languages: English
GDP: $1.376 trillion
Currency: Australian Dollar
Major Religions: Christianity
Government: Federal Parliamentary Constitutional Monarchy
Geography: Temperate, Desert, Savanna
Time Zone: UTC+8,+9:30,+!0
Major Cities: Sydney, Melbourne, Brisbane, Perth, Adelaide

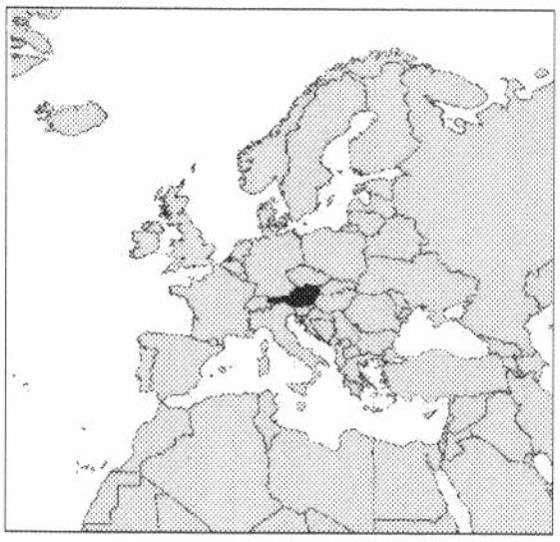

Austria in Europe

AUSTRIA

Capital City: Vienna
Area: 83,879 km² (32,386 sq mi)
Population: 8,857,960
Highest Point: Grobglockner (3798m)
Official Languages: German
GDP: $477.67 billion
Currency: Euro
Major Religions: Christianity
Government: Federal Parliamentary Republic
Geography: Mountain, Temperate
Time Zone: UTC+1
Major Cities: Vienna, Graz, Linz, Salzburg

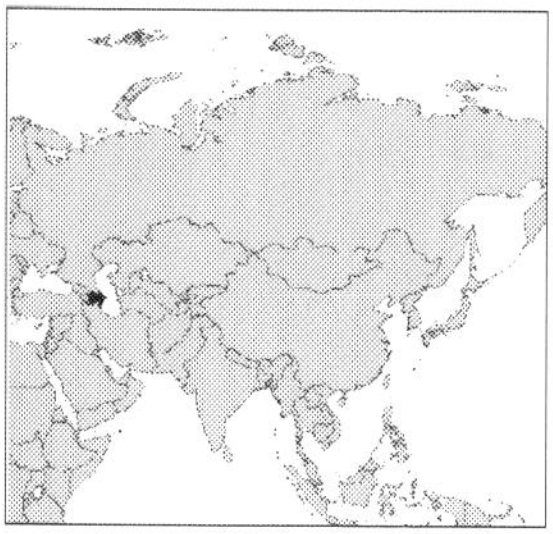

Azerbaijan in Europe/Asia

AZERBAIJAN

Capital City: Baku
Area: 86,600km² (33,400 sq mi)
Population: 10,000,000
Highest Point: Mt. Bazarduzu (4466m)
Official Languages: Azerbaijani
GDP: $45.28 billion
Currency: Manat
Major Religions: Islam
Government: Unitary Semi-Presidential Republic
Geography: Mountain, Temperate
Time Zone: UTC+3
Major Cities: Baku, Sumqayit, Ganja

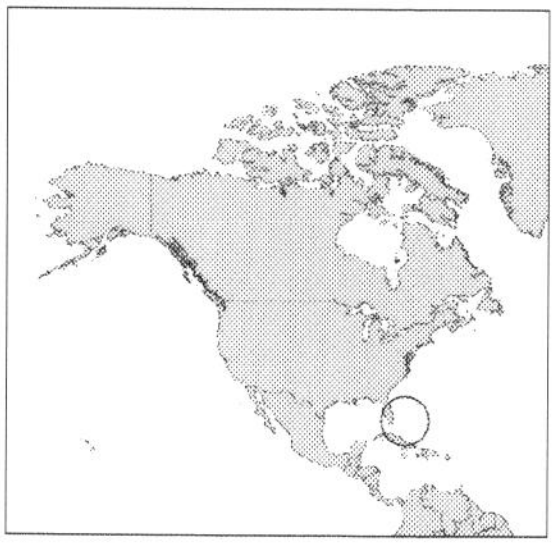

The Bahamas in North America

BAHAMAS, THE

Capital City: Nassau
Area: 13,878km² (5358 sq mi)
Population: 391,232
Highest Point: Mt. Alvernia (63m)
Official Languages: English
GDP: $12.80 billion
Currency: Bahamian Dollar
Major Religions: Christian
Government: Unitary Parliamentary Constitutional Monarchy
Geography: Tropical
Time Zone: UTC-5
Major Cities: Nassau

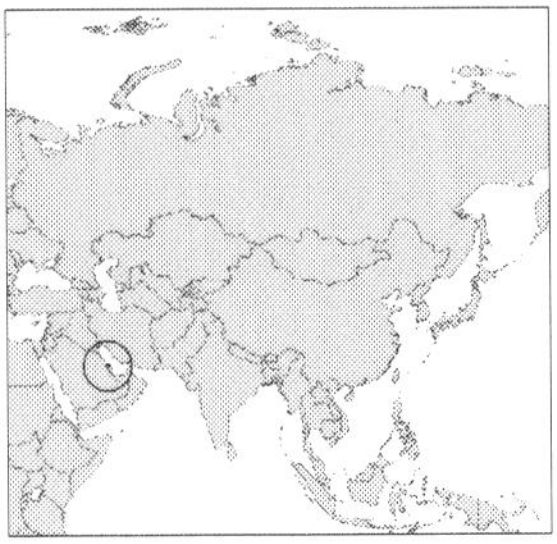

Bahrain in Asia

BAHRAIN

Capital City: Manama
Area: 778.3 km² (300.5 sq mi)
Population: 1,425,171
Highest Point: Mountain of Smoke (134m)
Official Languages: Arabic
GDP: $477.67 billion
Currency: Bahraini Dollar
Major Religions: Islam
Government: Unitary Parliamentary Islamic Constitutional Monarchy
Geography: Desert
Time Zone: UTC+3
Major Cities: Manama

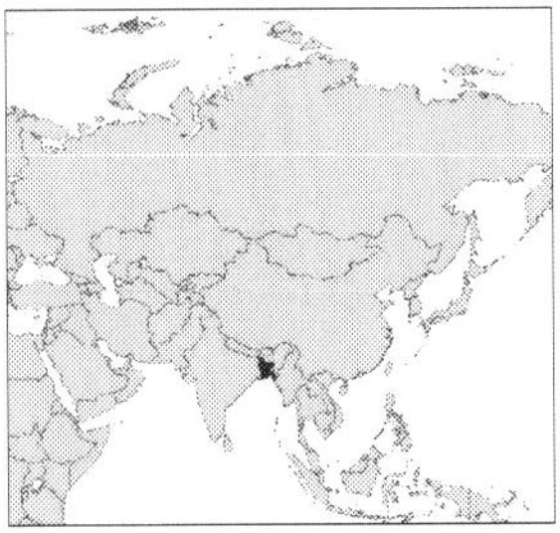

Bangladesh in Asia

BANGLADESH

Capital City: Dhaka
Area: 147,050km² (56,980 sq mi)
Population: 162,951,560
Highest Point: Keokradong (1064m)
Official Languages: Bengali
GDP: $317.47 billion
Currency: Bangladeshi Taka
Major Religions: Islam
Government: Unitary Parliamentary Constitutional Republic
Geography: Tropical
Time Zone: UTC+6
Major Cities: Dhaka, Chittagong

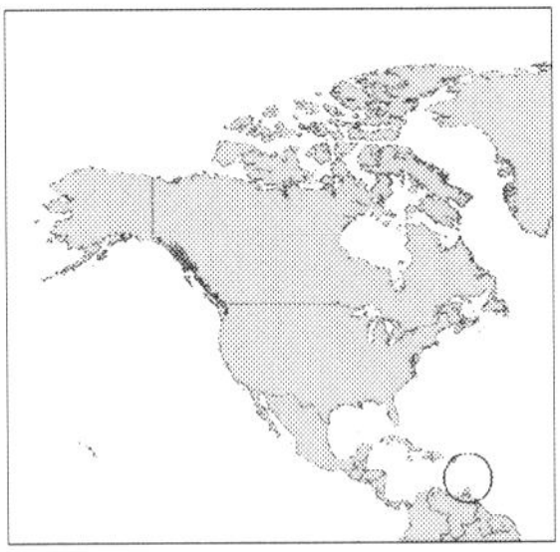

Barbados in North America

BARBADOS

Capital City: Bridgetown
Area: 439km² (169 sq mi)
Population: 272,821
Highest Point: Mt. Hillaby (340m)
Official Languages: English
GDP: $5.21 billion
Currency: Barbadian Dollar
Major Religions: Christian
Government: Unitary Parliamentary Constitutional Monarhcy
Geography: Tropical
Time Zone: UTC-4
Major Cities: Bridgetown

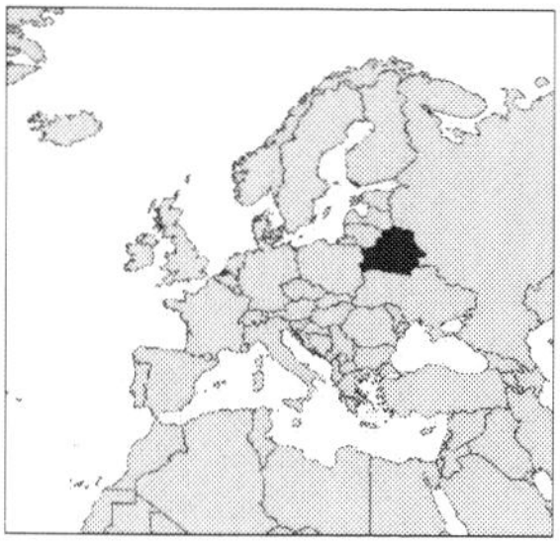

Belarus in Europe

BELARUS

Capital City: Minsk
Area: 207,595km² (80,153 sq mi)
Population: 9,491,800
Highest Point: Dzyarzhynsk Hill (345m)
Official Languages: Belarusian/Russian
GDP: $60.00 billion
Currency: Belarusian Ruble
Major Religions: Christianity, Irreligion
Government: Unitary Presidential Republic
Geography: Temperate
Time Zone: UTC+3
Major Cities: Minsk, Homyel, Mahilyow

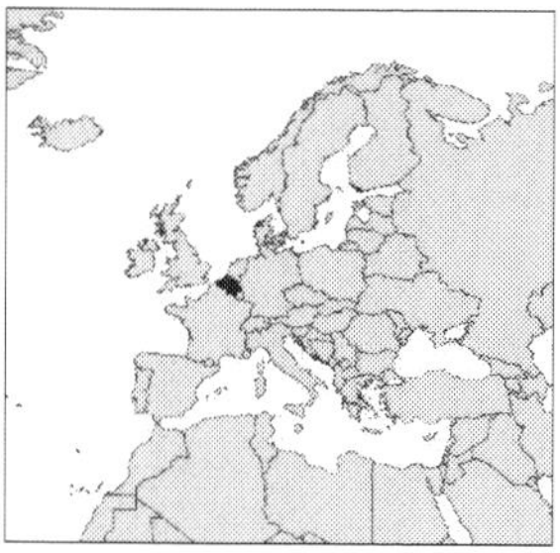

Belgium in Europe

BELGIUM

Capital City: Brussels
Area: 30,688 km² (11,849 sq mi)
Population: 11,420,163
Highest Point: Signal De Botrange (694m)
Official Languages: Dutch/French/German
GDP: $533.00 billion
Currency: Euro
Major Religions: Christianity, Irreligion
Government: Federal Parliamentary Constitutional Monarchy
Geography: Temperate
Time Zone: UTC+1
Major Cities: Brussels, Antwerp, Ghent

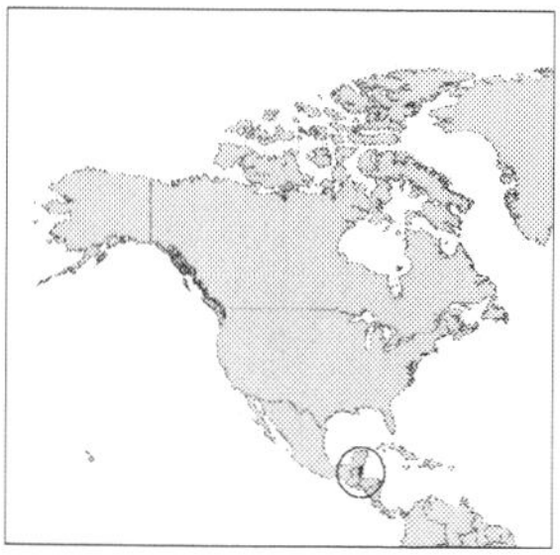

Belize in North America

BELIZE

Capital City: Belmopan
Area: 22,966 km² (8867 sq mi)
Population: 398,050
Highest Point: Doyle's Delight (1124m)
Official Languages: English
GDP: $1.987 billion
Currency: Belize Dollar
Major Religions: Christianity
Government: Unitary Parliamentary Constitutional Monarchy
Geography: Tropical
Time Zone: UTC-6
Major Cities: Belize City, Belmopan

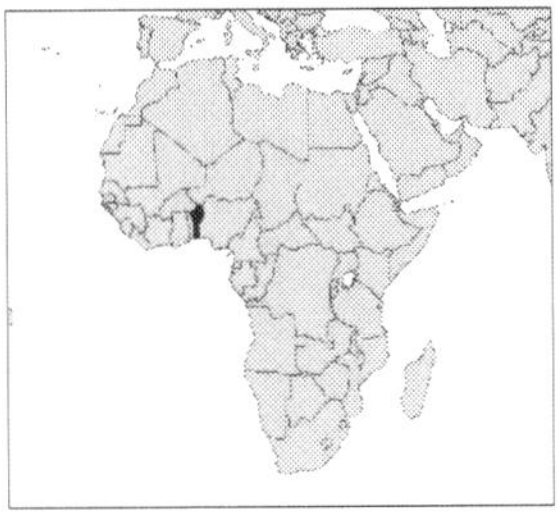

Benin in Africa

BENIN

Capital City: Porto-Novo
Area: 114,763 km² (44,310 sq mi)
Population: 10,872,298
Highest Point: Mt. Sokbaro (658m)
Official Languages: French
GDP: $10.56 billion
Currency: West African CFA Franc
Major Religions: Christianity, Islam
Government: Unitary Presidential Republic
Geography: Tropical, Savanna
Time Zone: UTC+1
Major Cities: Cotontau, Porto-Novo, Parakou, Godomey

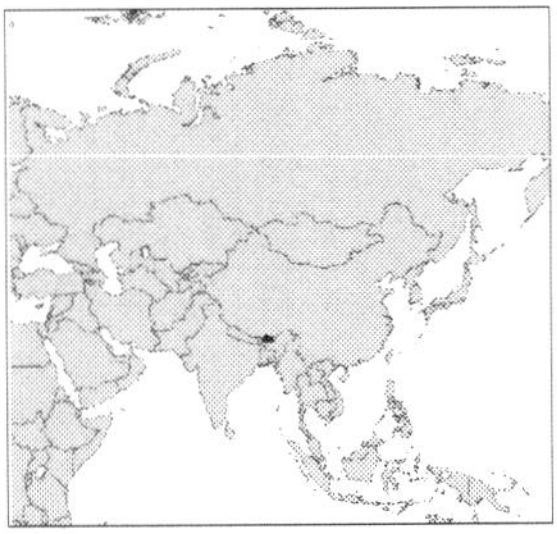

Bhutan in Asia

BHUTAN

Capital City: Thimphu
Area: 38,394km² (14,824 sq mi)
Population: 727,145
Highest Point: Gangkhar Puensum (7570m)
Official Languages: Dzongkha
GDP: $2.55 billion
Currency: Ngultrum
Major Religions: Buddhism, Hinduism
Government: Unitary Parliamentary Constitutional Monarchy
Geography: Mountain
Time Zone: UTC+6
Major Cities: Thimphu

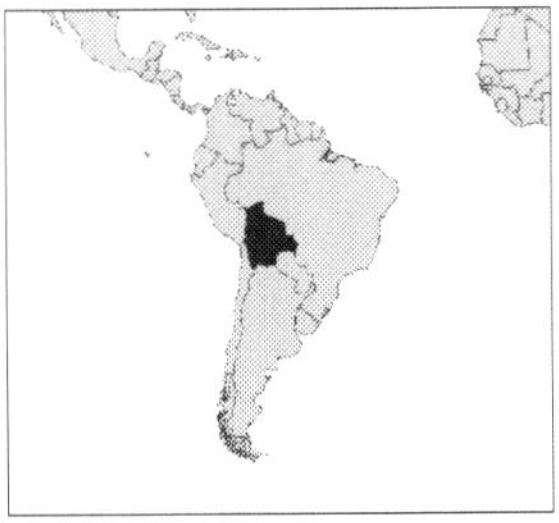

Bolivia in South America

BOLIVIA

Capital City: La Paz / Sucre
Area: 1,098,581 km² (424,164 sq mi)
Population: 11,428,245
Highest Point: Nevado Sajama (6542m)
Official Languages: Spanish (+36 others)
GDP: $43.69 billion
Currency: Boliviano
Major Religions: Christianity
Government: Unitary Presidential Constitutional Republic
Geography: Mountain, Tropical, Desert
Time Zone: UTC-4
Major Cities: Santa Cruz, El Alto, La Paz, Cochabamba

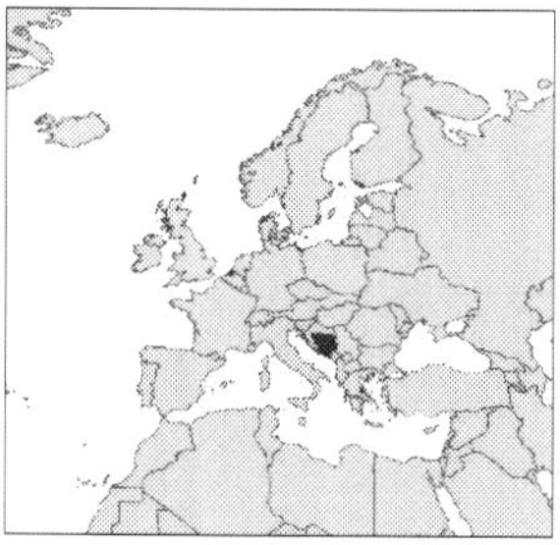

Bosnia and Herzegovina in Europe

BOSNIA AND HERZEGOVINA

Capital City: Sarajevo
Area: 51,129km² (19,741 sq mi)
Population: 3,511,372
Highest Point: Maglic (2386m)
Official Languages: (Bosnian/Serbian/ Croatian)
GDP: $20.72 billion
Currency: Convertible Mark
Major Religions: Islam, Christianity
Government: Federal Parliamentary Constitutional Republic
Geography: Mountain, Temperate
Time Zone: UTC+1
Major Cities: Sarajevo, Banja Luka

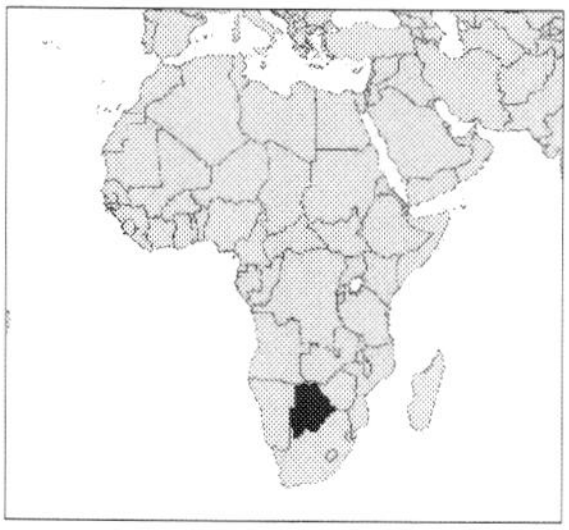

Botswana in Africa

BOTSWANA

Capital City: Gaborone
Area: 581,730km² (224,610 sq mi)
Population: 2,250,260
Highest Point: Monalanong Hill (1494m)
Official Languages: English/Setswana
GDP: $19.65 billion
Currency: Botswana Pula
Major Religions: Christianity
Government: Unitary Parliamentary Constitutional Republic
Geography: Desert
Time Zone: UTC+2
Major Cities: Gaborone, Francistown

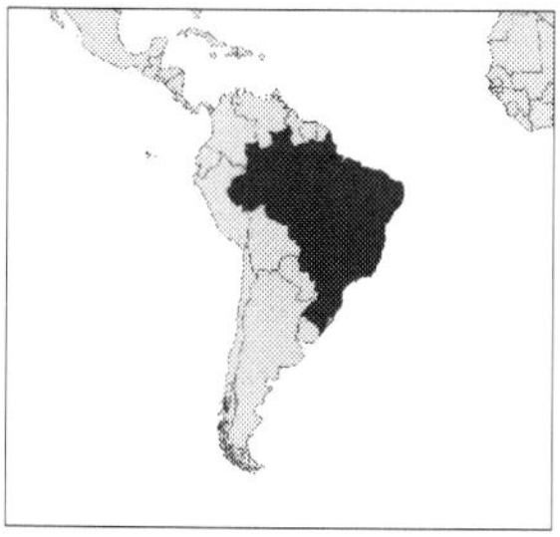

Brazil in South America

BRAZIL

Capital City: Brasilia
Area: 8,515,767km² (3,287,956 sq mi)
Population: 210,147,125
Highest Point: Pico de Neblina (2994m)
Official Languages: Portuguese
GDP: $1.847 trillion
Currency: Real
Major Religions: Christianity
Government: Federal Presidential Constitutional Republic
Geography: Tropical, Savanna, Temperate
Time Zone: UTC-5,-4,-3,-2
Major Cities: Rio De Janeiro, Sao Paulo, Belo Horizonte, Recife, Brasilia, Porto Alegre, Salvador

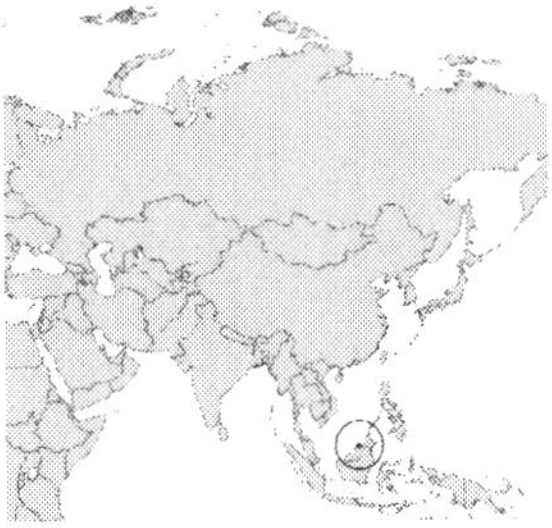

Brunei in Asia

BRUNEI

Capital City: Bandar Seri Begawan
Area: 5765 km² (2226 sq mi)
Population: 417,200
Highest Point: Bukit Pagon (1850m)
Official Languages: Malay
GDP: $13.33 billion
Currency: Brunei Dollar
Major Religions: Islam
Government: Unitary Islamic Absolute Monarchy
Geography: Tropical
Time Zone: UTC+8
Major Cities: Bandar Seri Begawan

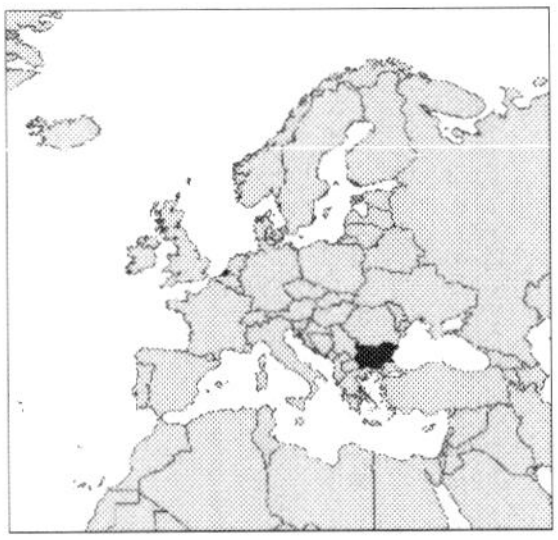

Bulgaria in Europe

BULGARIA

Capital City: Sofia
Area: 110,994km² (42,855sq mi)
Population: 7,050,034
Highest Point: Musala (2925m)
Official Languages: Bulgarian
GDP: $67.04 billion
Currency: Lev
Major Religions: Christianity
Government: Unitary Parliamentary Republic
Geography: Temperate
Time Zone: UTC+2
Major Cities: Sofia, Plovdiv, Varna

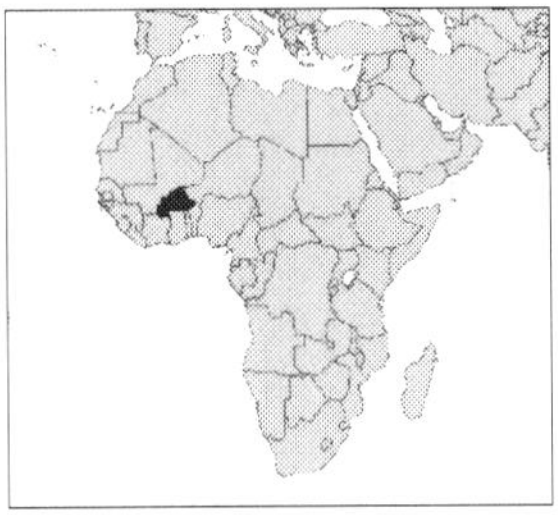

Burkina Faso in Africa

BURKINA FASO

Capital City: Ouagadougou
Area: 274,200km² (105,900 sq mi)
Population: 20,107,509
Highest Point: Tenakourou (749m)
Official Languages: French
GDP: $14.88 billion
Currency: West African CFA Franc
Major Religions: Islam
Government: Unitary Semi-Presidential Republic
Geography: Savanna, Desert
Time Zone: UTC+0
Major Cities: Ouagadougou, Bobo-Dioulasso

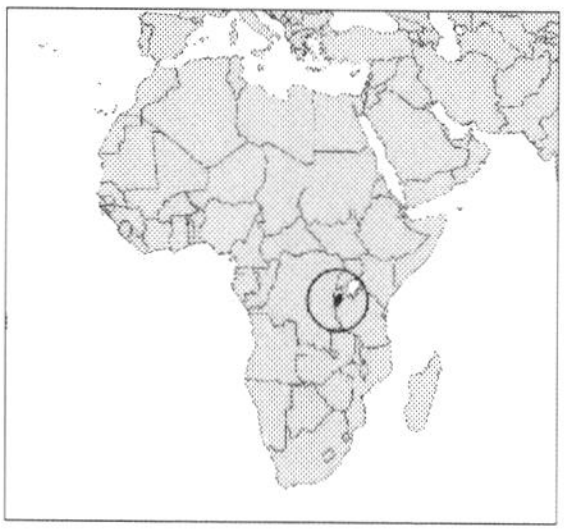

Burundi in Africa

BURUNDI

Capital City: Gitega
Area: 27,834km² (10,747 sq mi)
Population: 10,524,117
Highest Point: Mt. Heha (2685m)
Official Languages: English/French/Kirundi
GDP: $67.04 billion
Currency: Lev
Major Religions: Christianity
Government: Unitary Presidential Constitutional Republic
Geography: Tropical
Time Zone: UTC+2
Major Cities: Bujumbura

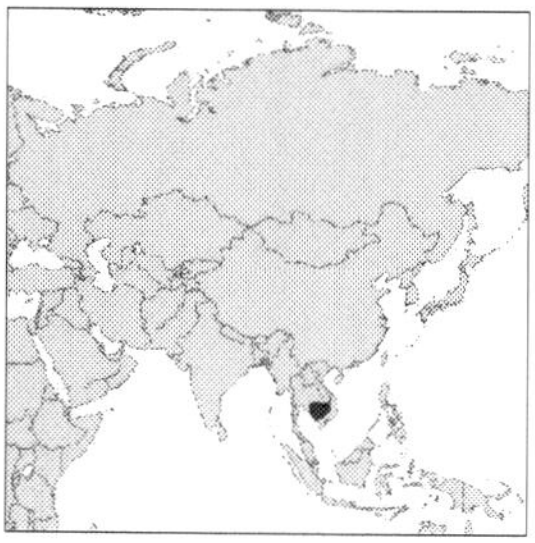

Cambodia in Asia

CAMBODIA

Capital City: Phnom Penh
Area: 181,035 km² (69,898 sq mi)
Population: 16,245,729
Highest Point: Phnom Aural (1813m)
Official Languages: Khmer
GDP: $24.36 billion
Currency: Riel
Major Religions: Buddhism
Government: Unitary Parliamental Constitutional Monarchy under a Dictatorship
Geography: Tropical
Time Zone: UTC+7
Major Cities: Phnom Penh, Ta Khmau

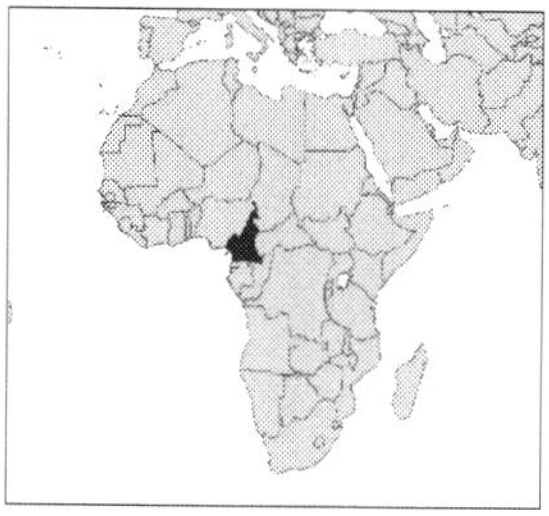

Cameroon in Africa

CAMEROON

Capital City: Yaounde
Area: 475,442km² (183,569 sq mi)
Population: 23,439,839
Highest Point: Mt. Cameroon (4095m)
Official Languages: English/French
GDP: $38.45 billion
Currency: Central African CFA Franc
Major Religions: Christianity
Government: Unitary Presidential Constitutional Republic
Geography: Savanna, Tropical
Time Zone: UTC+1
Major Cities: Douala, Yaounde, Bafoussam

CANADA

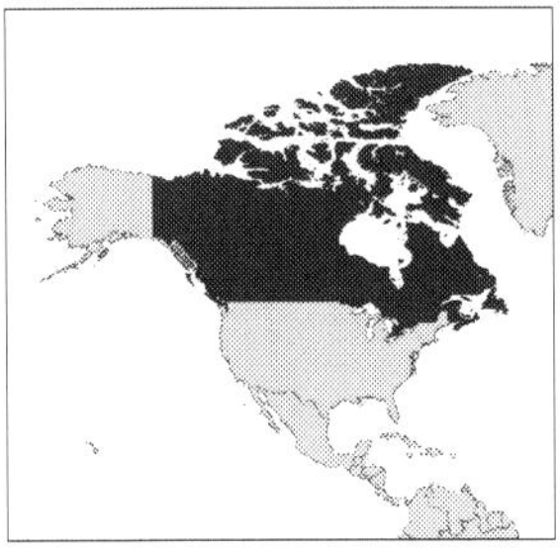

Canada in North America

Capital City: Ottawa
Area: 9,984,670km² (3,855,100 sq mi)
Population: 37,314,442
Highest Point: Mt. Logan (5959m)
Official Languages: English/French
GDP: $1.90 trillion
Currency: Canadian Dollar
Major Religions: Christianity
Government: Federal Parliamental Constitutional Monarchy
Geography: Temperate, Taiga, Tundra, Polar
Time Zone: UTC-8,-7,-6,-5,-4,-3:30
Major Cities: Toronto, Montreal, Vancouver, Calgary, Ottawa, Edmonton

CAPE VERDE (CABO VERDE)

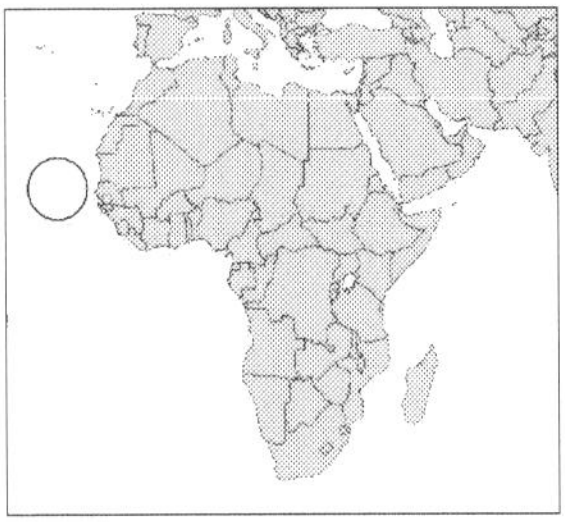

Cape Verde in Africa

Capital City: Praia
Area: 4033km² (1557 sq mi)
Population: 539,560
Highest Point: Mt. Fogo (2829m)
Official Languages: Portuguese
GDP: $2.04 billion
Currency: Cape Verdean Escudo
Major Religions: Christianity
Government: Unitary Semi-Presidential Republic
Geography: Desert
Time Zone: UTC-1
Major Cities: Praia

CENTRAL AFRICAN REPUBLIC

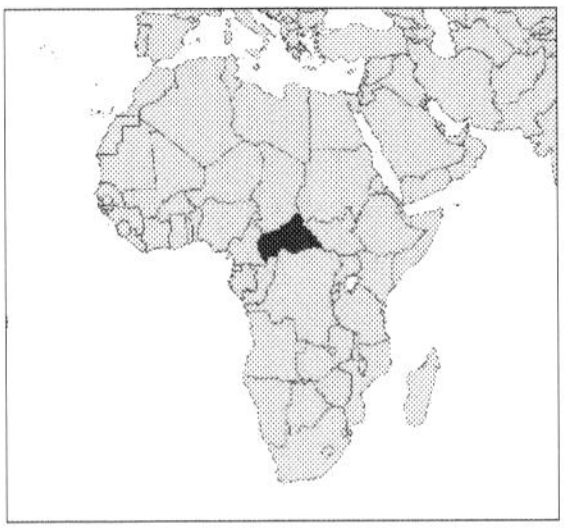

Central African Republic in Africa

Capital City: Bangui
Area: 622,984 km² (240,535 sq mi)
Population: 4,594,621
Highest Point: Mt. Ngaoui (1420m)
Official Languages: French/Sango
GDP: $2.00 billion
Currency: Central African CFA Franc
Major Religions: Christianity
Government: Unitary Semi-Presidential Constitutional Republic
Geography: Savanna
Time Zone: UTC+1
Major Cities: Bangui, Bimbo

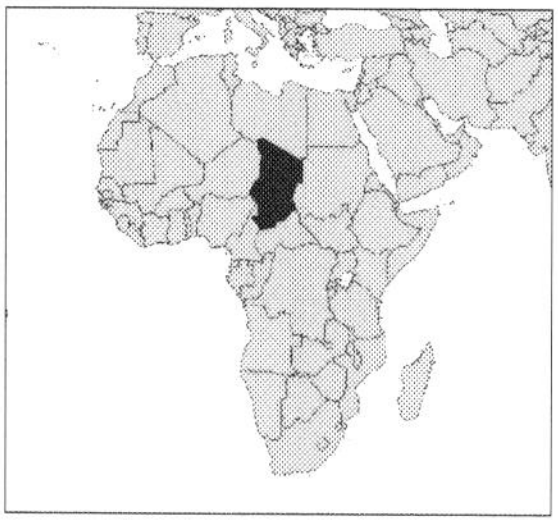

Chad in Africa

CHAD

Capital City: N'Djamena
Area: 1,284,000km² (496,000 sq mi)
Population: 8,857,960
Highest Point: Emi Koussi (3445m)
Official Languages: French/Arabic
GDP: $11.00 billion
Currency: Central African CFA Franc
Major Religions: Islam, Christianity
Government: Unitary Presidential Republic
Geography: Desert, Savanna
Time Zone: UTC+1
Major Cities: N'Djamena, Moundou

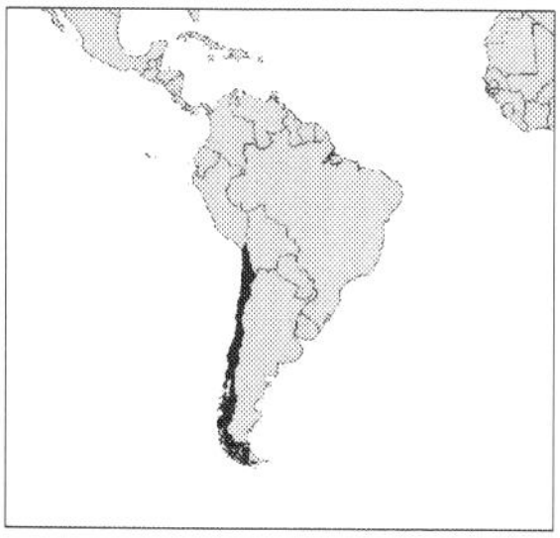

Chile in South America

CHILE

Capital City: Santiago
Area: 756,096km² (291,930 sq mi)
Population: 17,574,003
Highest Point: Ojos del Salado (6893m)
Official Languages: (Spanish)
GDP: $294.00 billion
Currency: Peso
Major Religions: Christianity
Government: Unitary Presidential Constitutional Republic
Geography: Desert, Temperate, Mountain
Time Zone: UTC-5,-3
Major Cities: Santiago, Valparaiso, Concepcion

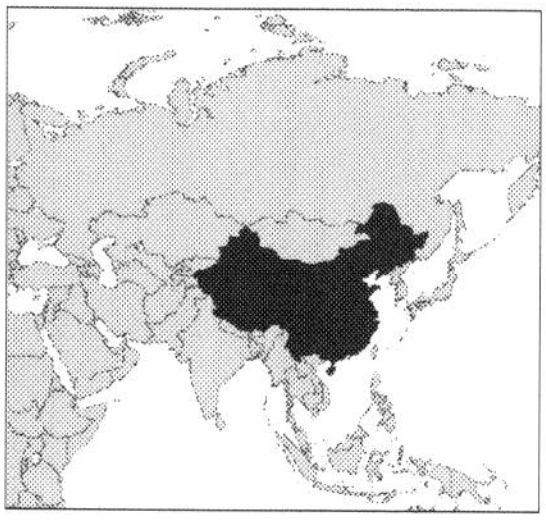

China in Asia

CHINA

Capital City: Beijing
Area: 9,596,961km² (3,705,407 sq mi)
Population: 1,403,500,365
Highest Point: Mt. Everest (8848m)
Official Languages: Standard Chinese
GDP: $14.21 trillion
Currency: Renminbi
Major Religions: Irreligious
Government: Unitary One Party Socialist Republic
Geography: Desert, Temperate, Mountain, Tundra, Tropical
Time Zone: UTC+8
Major Cities: Shanghai, Beijing, Chongqing, Guangzhou, Shenzhen, Tianjin, Wuhan, Dongguan, Hong Kong

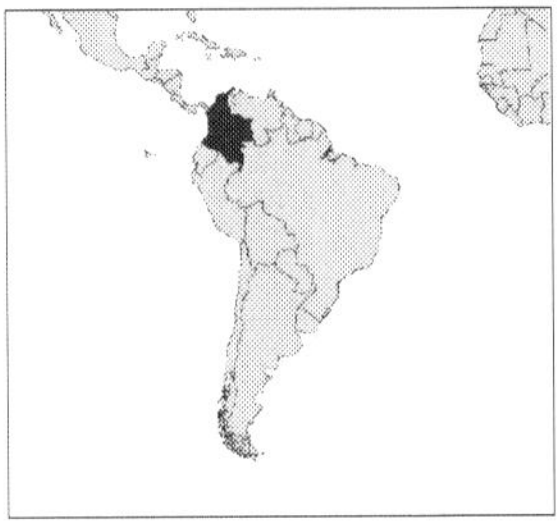

Colombia in South America

COLOMBIA

Capital City: Bogota
Area: 7,692,024 km² (2,969,907 sq mi)
Population: 25,330,200
Highest Point: Pico Cristobal Colon (5700m)
Official Languages: Spanish/English
GDP: $355.16 billion
Currency: Peso
Major Religions: Christianity
Government: Unitary Presidential Constitutional Republic
Geography: Tropical, Mountain
Time Zone: UTC-5,
Major Cities: Bogota, Medellin, Cali, Barranquilla

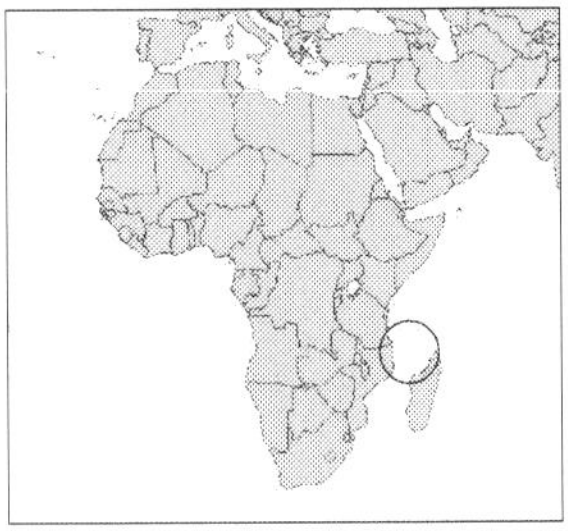

Comoros in Africa

COMOROS

Capital City: Moroni
Area: 1,659km² (641 sq mi)
Population: 850,688
Highest Point: Mt. Karthala (2360m)
Official Languages: Comorian/French/Arabic
GDP: $1.18 billion
Currency: Comorian Franc
Major Religions: Islam
Government: Federal Presidential Republic
Geography: Tropical
Time Zone: UTC+3
Major Cities: Moroni

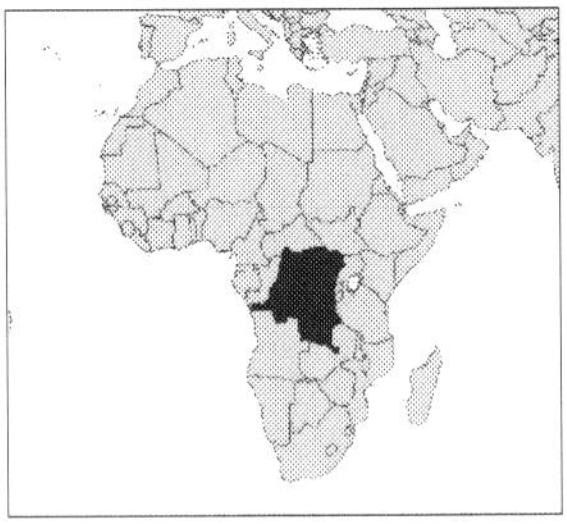

Democratic Republic of Congo in Africa

CONGO, DEMOCRATIC REPUBLIC OF

Capital City: Kinshasa
Area: 2,345,409km² (905,567 sq mi)
Population: 91,931,000
Highest Point: Mt. Stanley (5109m)
Official Languages: French
GDP: $77.12 trillion
Currency: Congolese Franc
Major Religions: Christianity
Government: Unitary Presidential Constitutional Republic
Geography: Savanna, Tropical, Mountain
Time Zone: UTC+1,+2
Major Cities: Kinshasa, Lubumbashi, Mbuji-Mayi

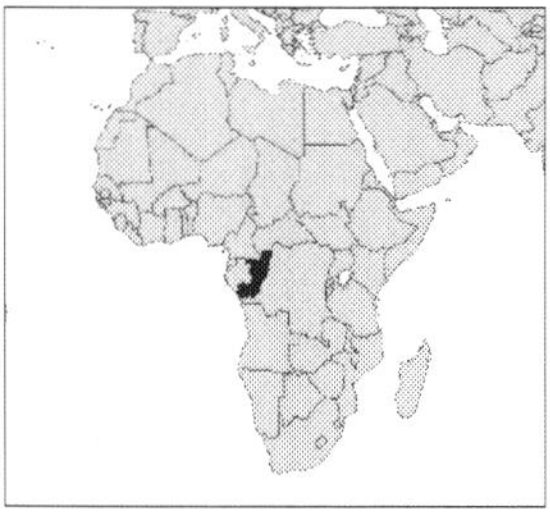

Republic of Congo in Africa

CONGO, REPUBLIC OF THE

Capital City: Brazzaville
Area: 342,000km² (132,000 sq mi)
Population: 5,121,821
Highest Point: Mt. Nabeba (1020m)
Official Languages: French
GDP: $11.16 billion
Currency: Central African CFA Franc
Major Religions: Christianity
Government: Unitary Presidential Republic
Geography: Tropical
Time Zone: UTC+1,
Major Cities: Brazzaville, Pointe-Noire

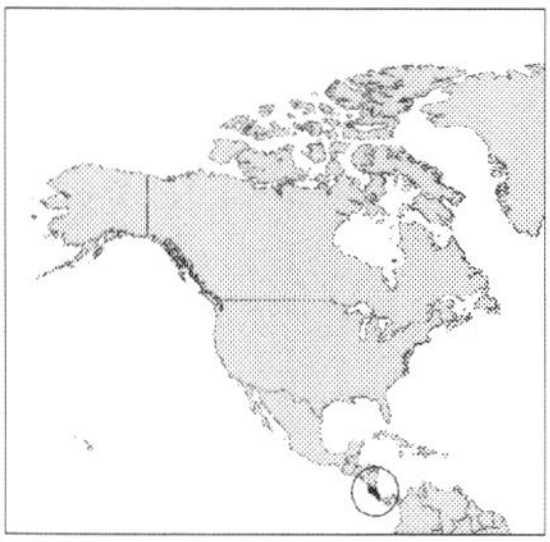

Costa Rica in North America

COSTA RICA

Capital City: San Jose
Area: 51,100km² (19,700 sq mi)
Population: 4,857,274
Highest Point: Cerro Chirripo (3820m)
Official Languages: Spanish
GDP: $61.02 billion
Currency: Costa Rican Colon
Major Religions: Christianity
Government: Unitary Presidential Constitutional Republic
Geography: Tropical
Time Zone: UTC-6
Major Cities: San Jose

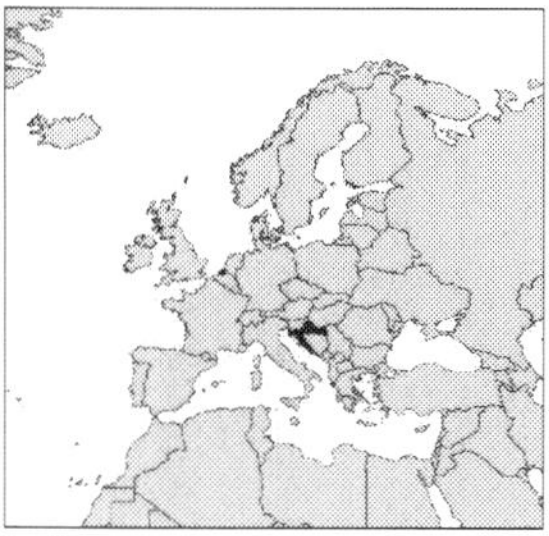

Croatia in Europe

CROATIA

Capital City: Zagreb
Area: 56,594km² (21,851 sq mi)
Population: 4,154,200
Highest Point: Dinara (1831m)
Official Languages: Croatian
GDP: $61.59 trillion
Currency: Kuna
Major Religions: Christianity
Government: Unitary Parliamental Constitutional Republic
Geography: Mediterranean, Temperate
Time Zone: UTC+1
Major Cities: Zagreb, Split, Rijeka

CUBA

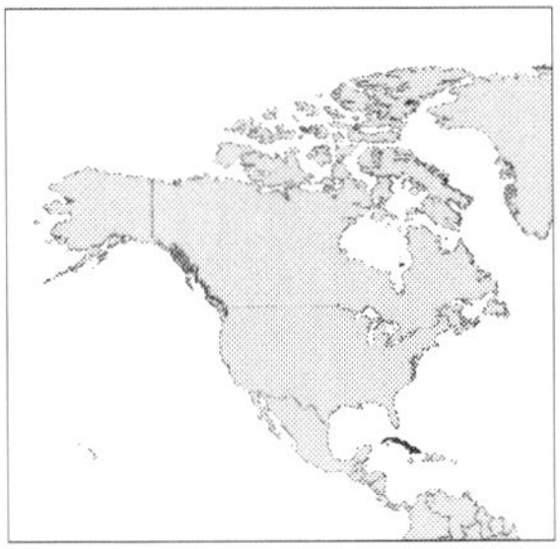

Cuba in North America

Capital City: Havana
Area: 109,884km² (42,426 sq mi)
Population: 11,221,060
Highest Point: Pico Turquino (1974m)
Official Languages: Spanish
GDP: $96.85 billion
Currency: Peso
Major Religions: Christianity
Government: Unitary Marxist-Leninist One-Party Socialist Republic
Geography: Tropical
Time Zone: UTC-5
Major Cities: Havana, Santiago de Cuba, Camaguey, Holguin

CYPRUS

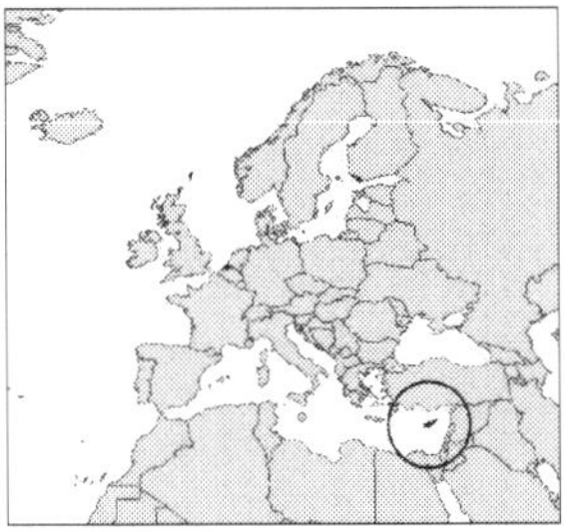

Cyprus in Europe

Capital City: Nicosia
Area: 9251km² (3572 sq mi)
Population: 1,170,125
Highest Point: Mt. Olympus (1951m)
Official Languages: Greek/Turkish
GDP: $25.00 billion
Currency: Euro
Major Religions: Christianity
Government: Unitary Presidential Constitutional Republic
Geography: Mediterranean
Time Zone: UTC+2
Major Cities: Nicosia, Limassol

CZECHIA

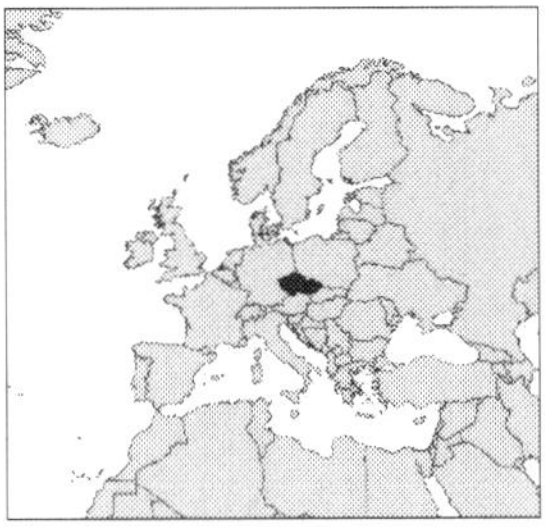

Czechia in Europe

Capital City: Prague
Area: 78,866 km² (30,450 sq mi)
Population: 10,610,947
Highest Point: Snezka (1603m)
Official Languages: Czech
GDP: $246.95 billion
Currency: Euro
Major Religions: Irreligion
Government: Unitary Parliamental Constitutional Republic
Geography: Temperate
Time Zone: UTC+1
Major Cities: Prague, Brno, Ostrava

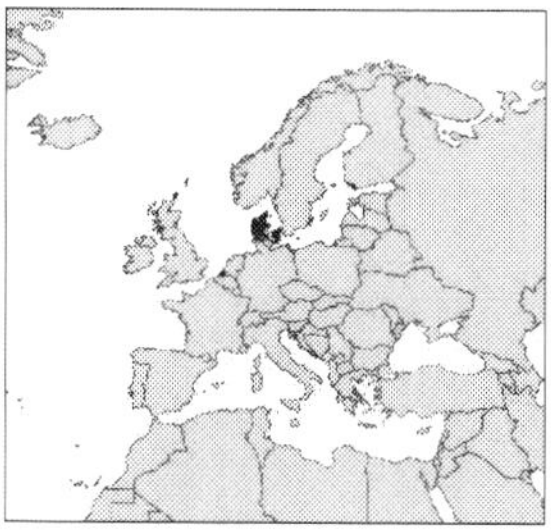

Denmark in Europe

DENMARK

Capital City: Copenhagen
Area: 42,933km^2 (32,386 sq mi)
Population: 5,806,015
Highest Point: Mollehoj (171m)
Official Languages: Danish
GDP: $96.85 billion
Currency: Euro
Major Religions: Christianity
Government: Unitary Parliamentary Constitutional Monarchy
Geography: Temperate
Time Zone: UTC+1
Major Cities: Copenhagen, Aarhus, Odense

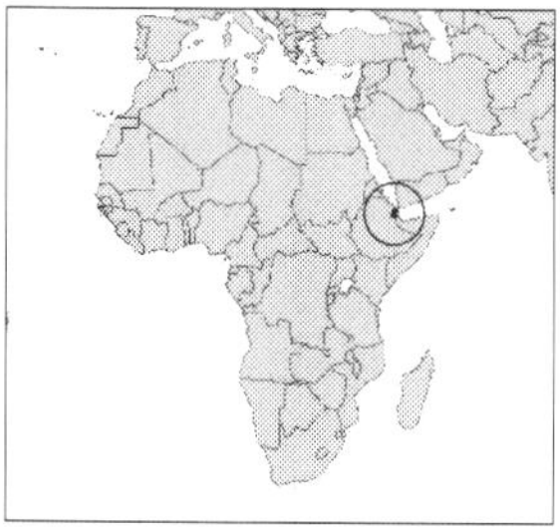

Djibouti in Africa

DJIBOUTI

Capital City: Djibouti City
Area: 23,200km^2 (9000 sq mi)
Population: 884,017
Highest Point: Mousa Ali (2028m)
Official Languages: French/Arabic
GDP: $2.19 billion
Currency: Djiboutian Franc
Major Religions: Islam
Government: Unitary Presidential Republic Under A Dictatorship
Geography: Desert
Time Zone: UTC+3
Major Cities: Djibouti City

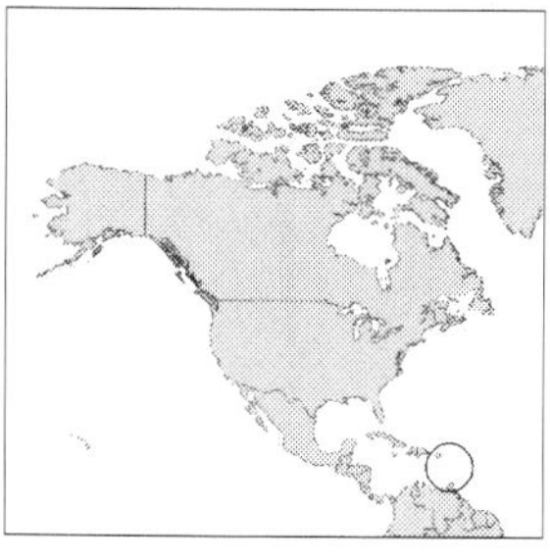

Dominica in North America

DOMINICA

Capital City: Roseau
Area: 750km^2 (290 sq mi)
Population: 73,543
Highest Point: Morne Diablotins (1447m)
Official Languages: English
GDP: $0.49 billion
Currency: Eastern Caribbean Dollar
Major Religions: Christianity
Government: Unitary Parliamentary Republic
Geography: Tropical
Time Zone: UTC-4
Major Cities: Roseau

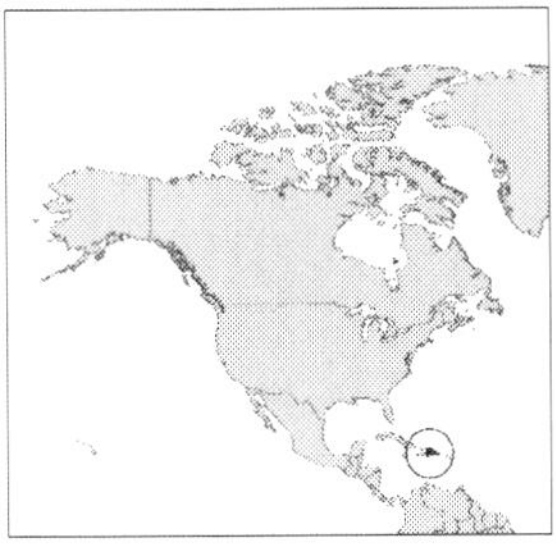

Dominican Republic in North America

DOMINICAN REPUBLIC

Capital City: Santo Domingo
Area: 48,671 km² (18,792 sq mi)
Population: 10,735,896
Highest Point: Pico Duarte (3098m)
Official Languages: Spanish
GDP: $86.57 billion
Currency: Peso
Major Religions: Christianity
Government: Unitary Presidential Republic
Geography: Tropical
Time Zone: UTC-4
Major Cities: Santo Domingo, Santiago

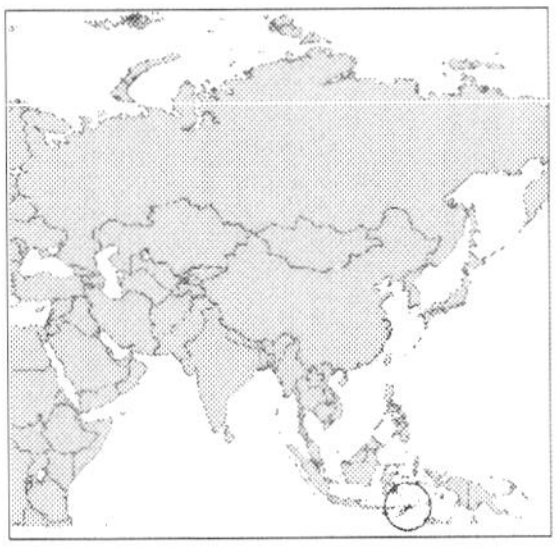

East Timor in Asia

EAST TIMOR (TIMOR-LESTE)

Capital City: Dili
Area: 15,007km² (5794 sq mi)
Population: 1,167,242
Highest Point: Mt. Ramelau (2963m)
Official Languages: Portuguese/Tetum
GDP: $3.145 billion
Currency: United States Dollar
Major Religions: Christianity
Government: Unitary Presidential Constitutional Republic
Geography: Tropical
Time Zone: UTC+9
Major Cities: Dili

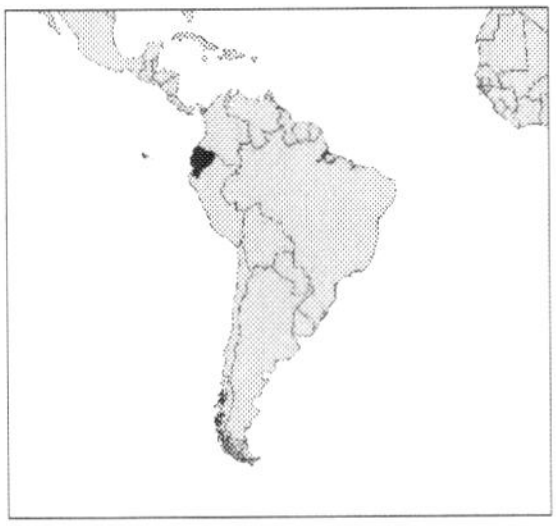

Ecuador in South America

ECUADOR

Capital City: Quito
Area: 283,561km² (109,484 sq mi)
Population: 16,385,068
Highest Point: Chimborazo (6267m)
Official Languages: Spanish
GDP: $106.29 billion
Currency: United States Dollar
Major Religions: Christianity
Government: Unitary Presidential Constitutional Republic
Geography: Tropical, Mountain
Time Zone: UTC-6,-5
Major Cities: Guayaquil, Quito

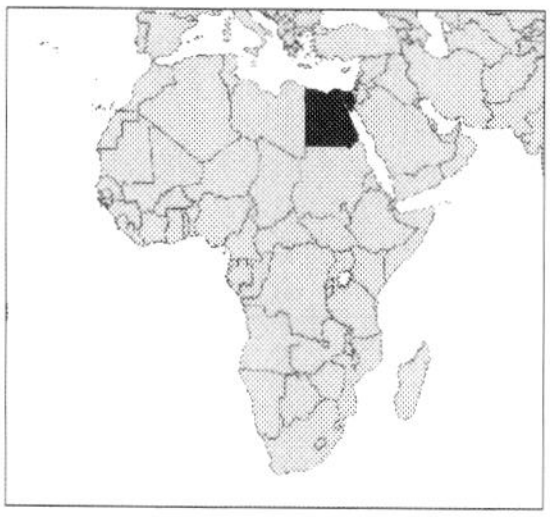

Egypt in Africa

EGYPT

Capital City: Cairo
Area: 1,010,408km^2 (390,121 sq mi)
Population: 94,798,827
Highest Point: Mt. Catherine (2629m)
Official Languages: Arabic
GDP: $302.25 billion
Currency: Egyptian Pound
Major Religions: Islam
Government: Unitary Presidential Republic
Geography: Desert
Time Zone: UTC+2
Major Cities: Cairo, Alexandria, Giza, Shubra El Kheima, Port Said, Suez

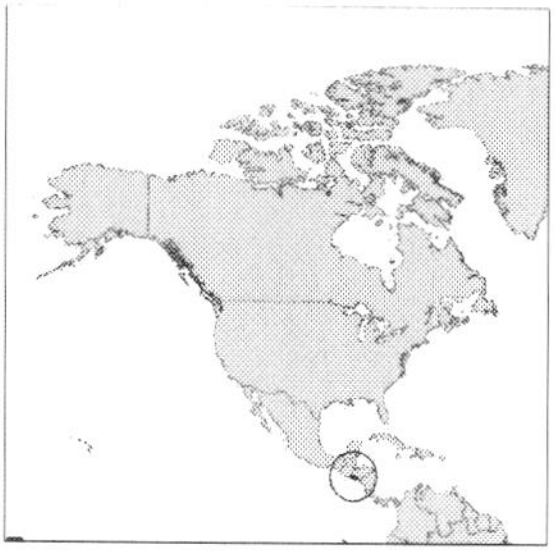

El Salvador in North America

EL SALVADOR

Capital City: San Salvador
Area: 21,041 km^2 (8124 sq mi)
Population: 6,344,722
Highest Point: Cerro El Pital (2730m)
Official Languages: Spanish
GDP: $25.86 billion
Currency: United States Dollar
Major Religions: Christianity
Government: Unitary Presidential Constitutional Republic
Geography: Tropical
Time Zone: UTC-6
Major Cities: San Salvador, Santa Ana, Soyapango

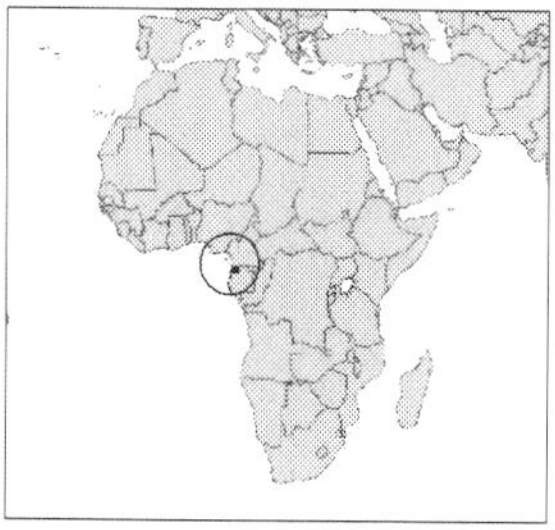

Equatorial Guinea in Africa

EQUATORIAL GUINEA

Capital City: Malabo
Area: 28,050km^2 (10,830 sq mi)
Population: 1,221,490
Highest Point: Pico Basile (3008m)
Official Languages: Spanish/French/Portuguese
GDP: $12.43 billion
Currency: Central African CFA Franc
Major Religions: Christianity
Government: Unitary Presidential Constitutional Republic
Geography: Tropical
Time Zone: UTC+1
Major Cities: Malabo, Bata

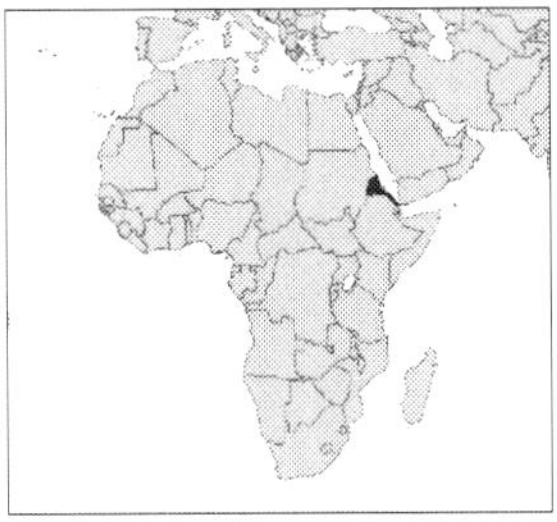

Eritrea in Africa

ERITREA

Capital City: Asmara
Area: 117,600km² (45,400 sq mi)
Population: 4,954,645
Highest Point: Embe Soira (3018m)
Official Languages: (16 other languages)
GDP: $7.72 billion
Currency: Nakfa
Major Religions: Christianity, Islam
Government: Unitary One-Party Presidential Republic
Geography: Desert, Mountain
Time Zone: UTC+3
Major Cities: Asmara, Keren

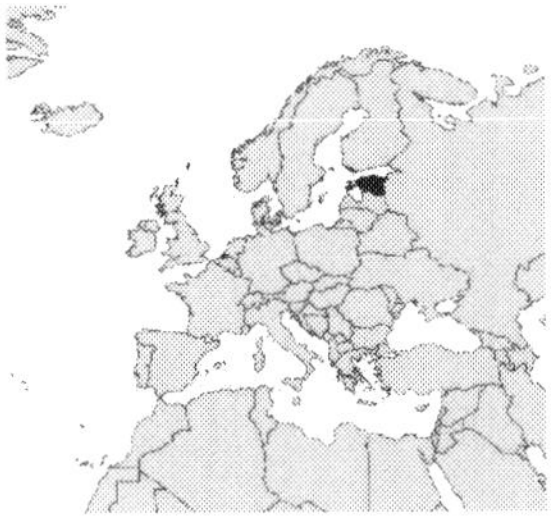

Estonia in Europe

ESTONIA

Capital City: Tallinn
Area: 45,227km² (17,462 sq mi)
Population: 1,324,820
Highest Point: Suur Mugamani (318m)
Official Languages: Estonian
GDP: $31.04 billion
Currency: Euro
Major Religions: Christianity, Irreligious
Government: Unitary Parliamentary Republic
Geography: Temperate
Time Zone: UTC+2
Major Cities: Tallinn, Tartu

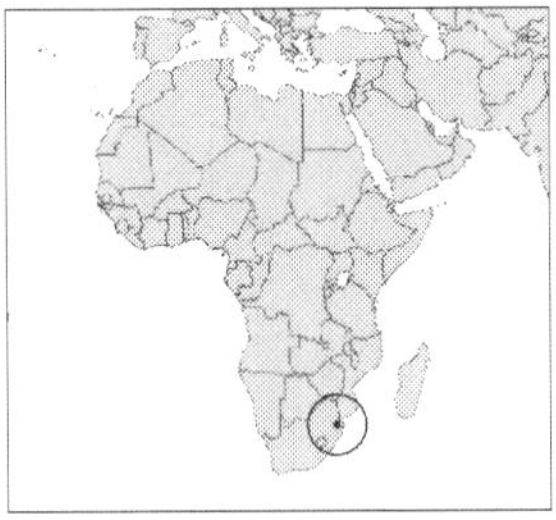

Eswatini in Africa

ESWATINI

Capital City: Mbabane
Area: 17,364 km² (6704 sq mi)
Population: 1,343,098
Highest Point: Emlembe (1862m)
Official Languages: English/Swazi
GDP: $4.66 billion
Currency: Swazi liliangeni/South African Rand
Major Religions: Christianity
Government: Unitary Parliamentary Absolute Monarchy
Geography: Mountain, Tropical, Savanna
Time Zone: UTC+2
Major Cities: Mbabane

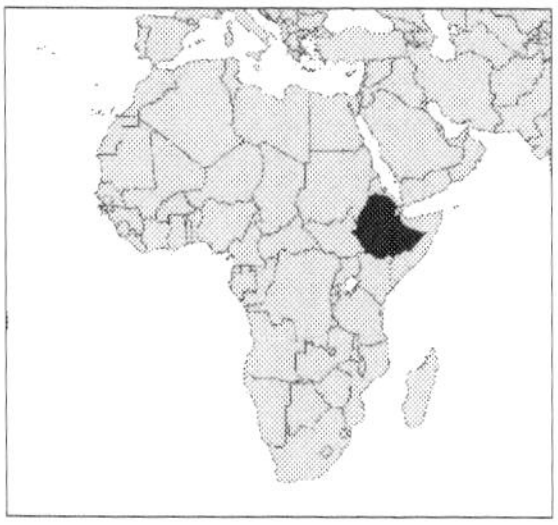

Ethiopia in Africa

ETHIOPIA

Capital City: Addis Ababa
Area: 1,104,300km² (426,400 sq mi)
Population: 102,403,196
Highest Point: Ras Dejen (4550m)
Official Languages: Amharic
GDP: $91.17 billion
Currency: Birr
Major Religions: Christianity, Islam
Government: Federal Parliamentary Constitutional Republic
Geography: Desert, Mountain, Tropical, Savanna
Time Zone: UTC+3
Major Cities: Addis Ababa, Adama, Gondar, Mek'ele

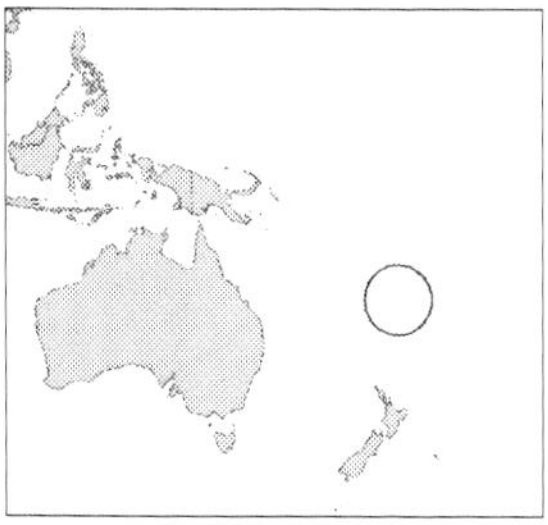

Fiji in Australia & Oceania

FIJI

Capital City: Suva
Area: 18,274km² (7056 sq mi)
Population: 912,241
Highest Point: Tomanivi (1324m)
Official Languages: English/Fijian/Fiji Hindi
GDP: $5.22 billion
Currency: Fijian Dollar
Major Religions: Christianity, Hinduism
Government: Unitary Parliamentary Constitutional Republic
Geography: Tropical
Time Zone: UTC+2
Major Cities: Suva

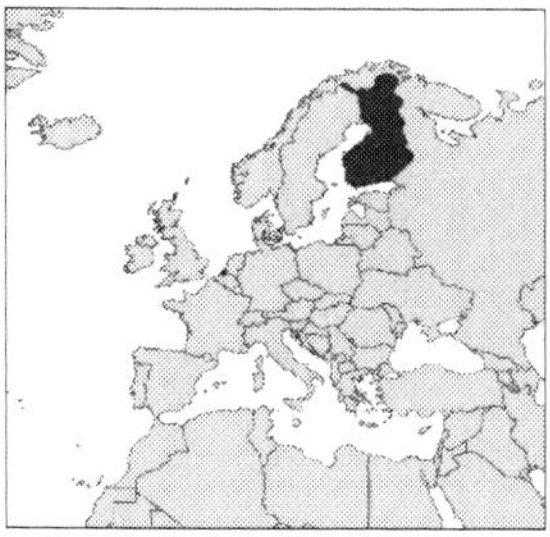

Finland in Europe

FINLAND

Capital City: Helsinki
Area: 338,424km² (130,666 sq mi)
Population: 5,519,586
Highest Point: Halti (1324m)
Official Languages: Finnish/Swedish
GDP: $277.00 billion
Currency: Euro
Major Religions: Christianity
Government: Unitary Parliamentary Republic
Geography: Temperate, Taiga, Tundra
Time Zone: UTC+2
Major Cities: Helsinki, Espoo, Tampere, Vantaa, Oulu, Turku

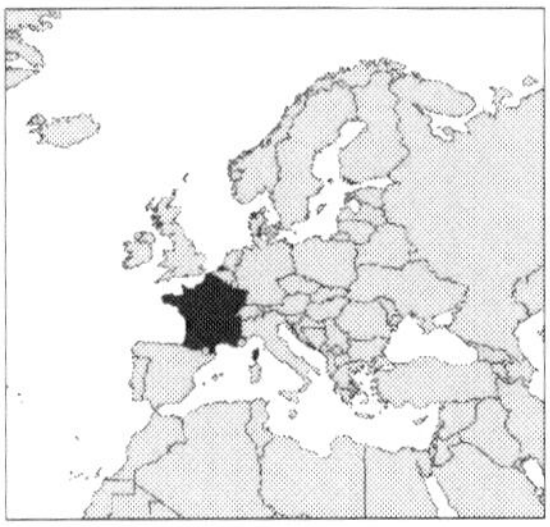

France in Europe

FRANCE

Capital City: Paris
Area: 640,679 km² (247,368 sq mi)
Population: 66,998,000
Highest Point: Mont Blanc (4810m)
Official Languages: French
GDP: $2707.00 billion
Currency: Euro
Major Religions: Christianity
Government: Unitary Presidential Republic
Geography: Temperate, Mediterannean, Mountain
Time Zone: UTC+1
Major Cities: Paris, Marseille, Lyon, Toulouse, Nice, Nantes, Montpellier, Strasbourg, Bordeaux, Lille

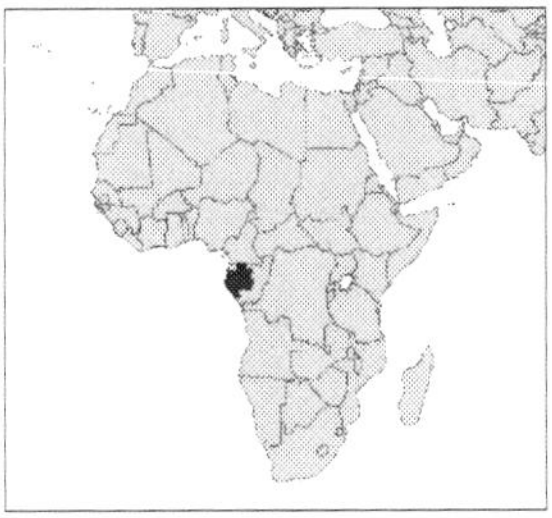

Gabon in Africa

GABON

Capital City: Libreville
Area: 267,667km² (103,347 sq mi)
Population: 1,979,786
Highest Point: Mont Bengoue (1070m)
Official Languages: French
GDP: $17.21 billion
Currency: Central African CFA Franc
Major Religions: Christianity
Government: Unitary Presidential Republic
Geography: Tropical, Savanna
Time Zone: UTC+1
Major Cities: Libreville, Port-Gentil, Franceville

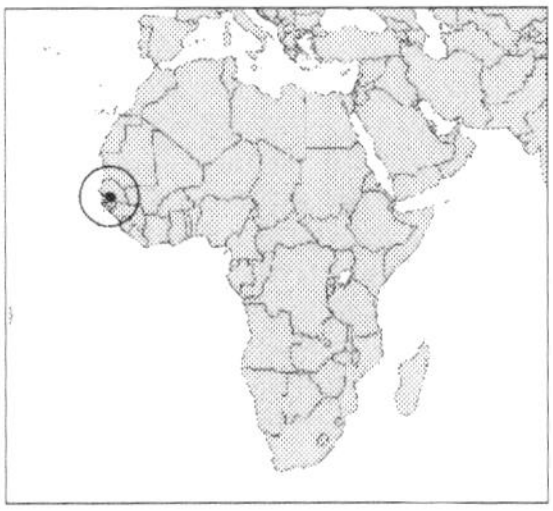

The Gambia in Africa

GAMBIA, THE

Capital City: Bangul
Area: 10,689km² (4127 sq mi)
Population: 2,051,363
Highest Point: Red Rock (53m)
Official Languages: English
GDP: $1.04 billion
Currency: Dalasi
Major Religions: Islam
Government: Unitary Presidential Republic
Geography: Savanna
Time Zone: UTC+0
Major Cities: Serekunda, Banjul

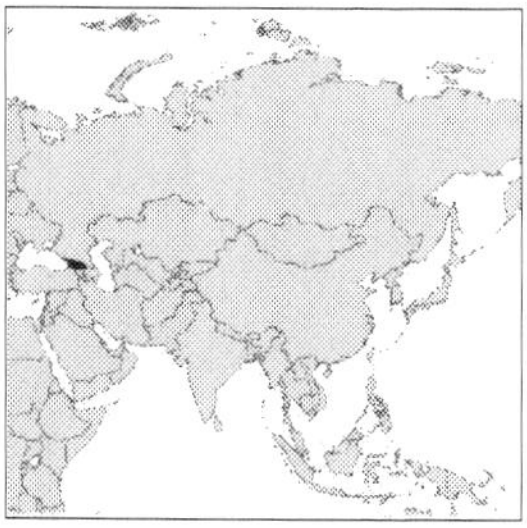

Georgia in Asia

GEORGIA

Capital City: Tbilisi
Area: 69,700m^2 (26,900 sq mi)
Population: 3,723,500
Highest Point: Shkhara (5201m)
Official Languages: Georgian/Abkhazian
GDP: $17.84 billion
Currency: Georgian lari
Major Religions: Christianity
Government: Unitary Parliamentary Constitutional Republic
Geography: Temperate, Mountain
Time Zone: UTC+4
Major Cities: Tbilisi, Batumi, Kutaisi, Rustavi

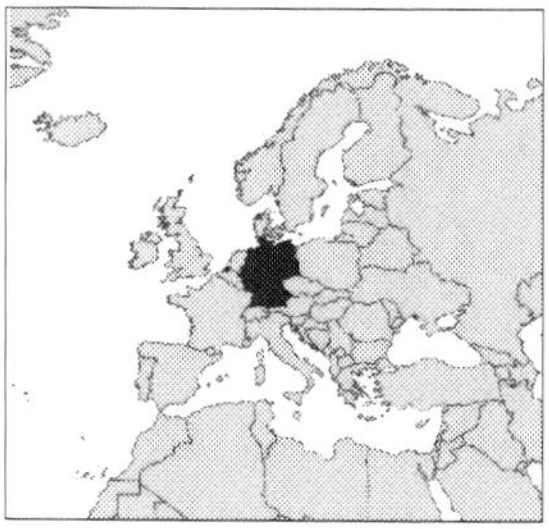

Germany in Europe

GERMANY

Capital City: Berlin
Area: 357,386 km^2 (137,988 sq mi)
Population: 83,019,200
Highest Point: Zugspitze (2962m)
Official Languages: German
GDP: $3863.00 billion
Currency: Euro
Major Religions: Christianity, Irelligious
Government: Federal Parliamentary Republic
Geography: Temperate
Time Zone: UTC+1
Major Cities: Berlin, Hamburg, Munich, Cologne, Frankfurt, Stuttgart, Dusseldorf, Leipzig

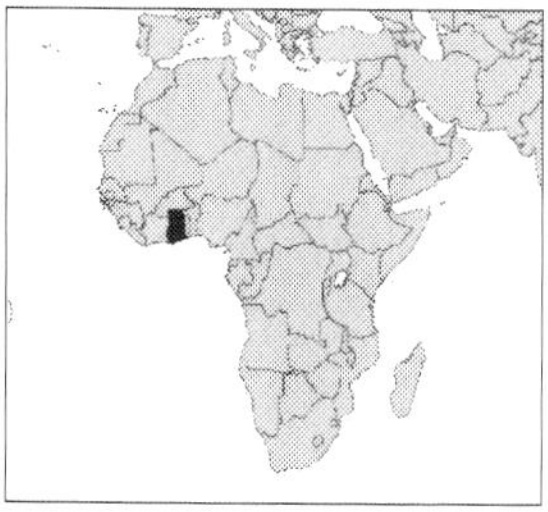

Ghana in Africa

GHANA

Capital City: Accra
Area: 239,567km^2 (92,497 sq mi)
Population: 28,308,301
Highest Point: Mt. Afadjato (880m)
Official Languages: English
GDP: $68.00 billion
Currency: Ghanaian Cedi
Major Religions: Christianity
Government: Unitary Presidential Constitutional Republic
Geography: Savanna, Tropical
Time Zone: UTC+0
Major Cities: Accra

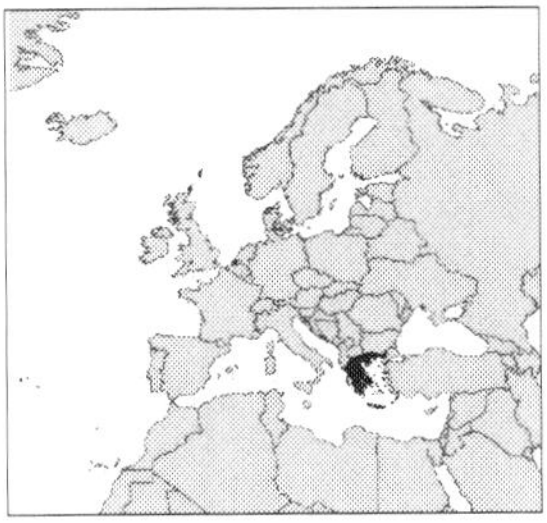

Greece in Europe

GREECE

Capital City: Athens
Area: 131,957km² (50,949 sq mi)
Population: 10,768,477
Highest Point: Mt. Olympus (2919m)
Official Languages: Greek
GDP: $214.00 billion
Currency: Euro
Major Religions: Christianity
Government: Unitary Parliamentary Republic
Geography: Mediterranean, Temperate
Time Zone: UTC+2
Major Cities: Athens, Thessaloniki, Patras, Larissa, Heraklion

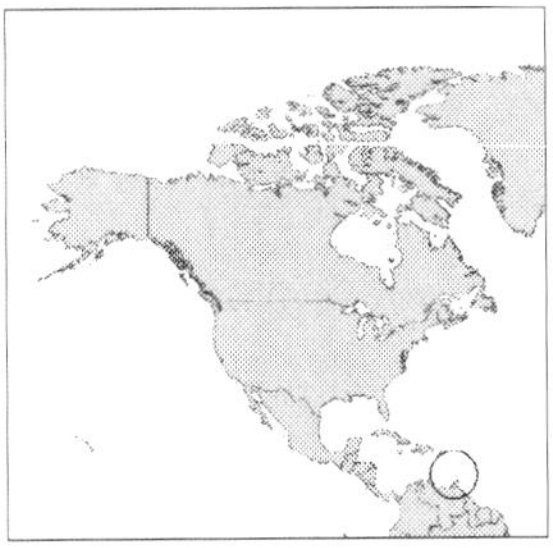

Grenada in North America

GRENADA

Capital City: St George's
Area: 349km² (135 sq mi)
Population: 107,317
Highest Point: Mt. Saint Catherine (840m)
Official Languages: English
GDP: $1.25 billion
Currency: East Caribbean Dollar
Major Religions: Christianity
Government: Unitary Two-Party Parliamentary Constitutional Monarchy
Geography: Tropical
Time Zone: UTC-4
Major Cities: St George's

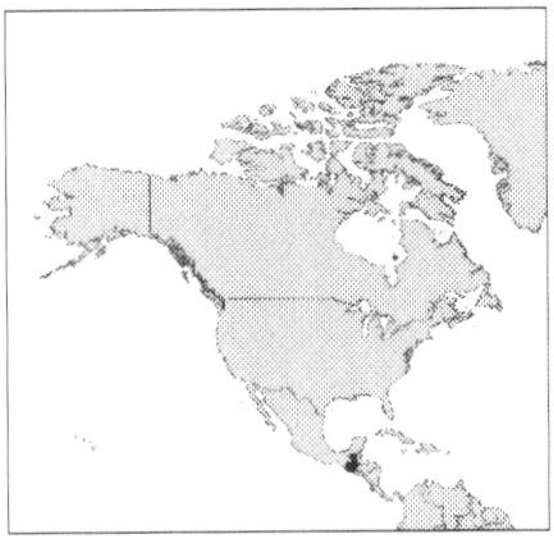

Guatemala in North America

GUATEMALA

Capital City: Guatemala City
Area: 108,889 km² (42,042 sq mi)
Population: 17,263,239
Highest Point: Volcan Tajumulco (4220m)
Official Languages: Spanish
GDP: $79.11 billion
Currency: Quetzal
Major Religions: Christianity
Government: Unitary Presidential Republic
Geography: Mountain, Tropical
Time Zone: UTC-6
Major Cities: Guatemala City, Mixco, Villa Nueva

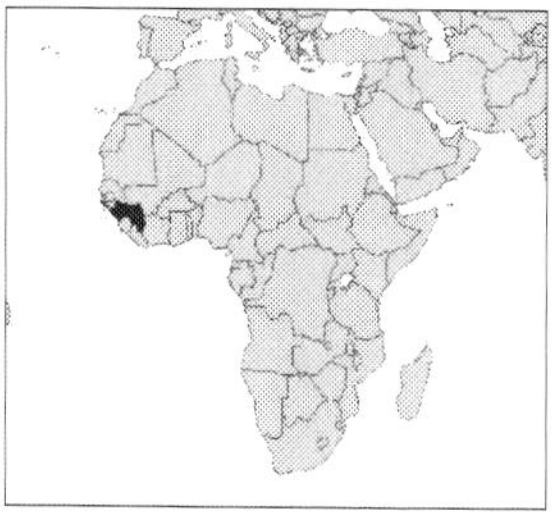

Guinea in Africa

GUINEA

Capital City: Conakry
Area: 245,836km² (94,918 sq mi)
Population: 12,395,924
Highest Point: Mont Nimba (1752m)
Official Languages: French
GDP: $9.18 billion
Currency: Guinean Franc
Major Religions: Islam
Government: Unitary Presidential Republic
Geography: Savanna, Tropical
Time Zone: UTC+0
Major Cities: Conakry, Nzerekore, Kankan

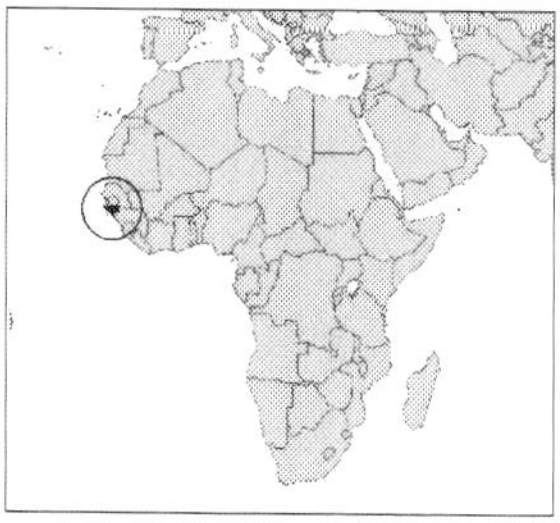

Guinea-Bissau in Africa

GUINEA-BISSAU

Capital City: Bissau
Area: 36,125km² (13,948 sq mi)
Population: 1,815,698
Highest Point: Unnamed (300m)
Official Languages: Portuguese
GDP: $1.48 billion
Currency: West African CFA Franc
Major Religions: Christianity, Islam
Government: Unitary Presidential Republic
Geography: Tropical, Savanna
Time Zone: UTC+0
Major Cities: Bissau

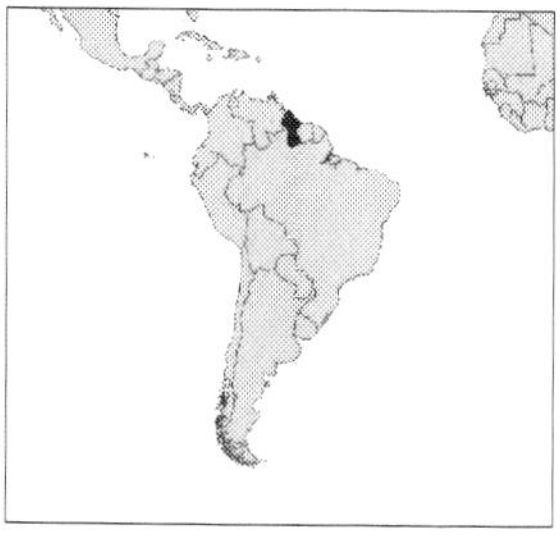

Guyana in South America

GUYANA

Capital City: Georgetown
Area: 214,970km² (83,000 sq mi)
Population: 783,769
Highest Point: Mt. Roraima (2772m)
Official Languages: English
GDP: $3.88 billion
Currency: Guyanese Dollar
Major Religions: Christianity, Hinduism
Government: Unitary Presidential Constitutional Socialist Republic
Geography: Tropical
Time Zone: UTC-4
Major Cities: Georgetown

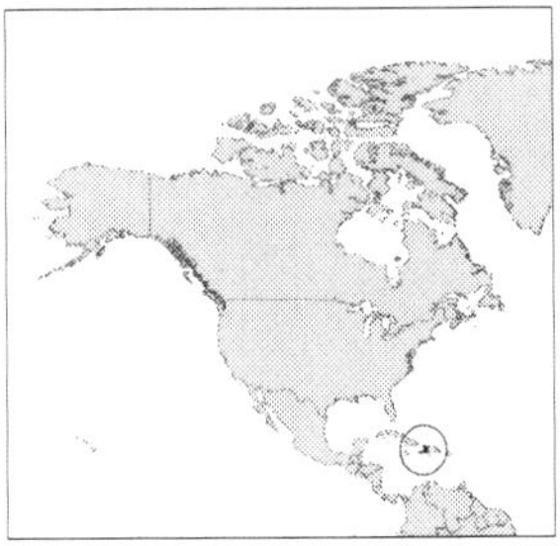

Haiti in North America

HAITI

Capital City: Port-Au-Prince
Area: 27,750 km² (10,710 sq mi)
Population: 10,847,334
Highest Point: Pic La Selle (2680m)
Official Languages: French/Haitian Creole
GDP: $7.90 billion
Currency: Haitian Gourde
Major Religions: Islam
Government: Unitary Presidential Republic
Geography: Tropical, Mountain
Time Zone: UTC-5
Major Cities: Port-Au-Prince, Cap-Haiten, Carrefour, Delmas

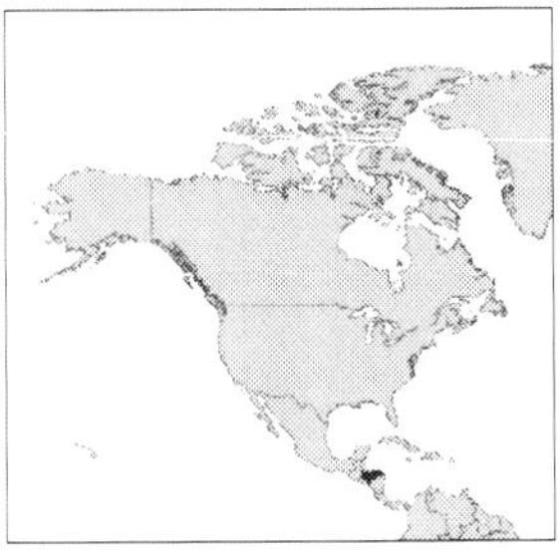

Honduras in North America

HONDURAS

Capital City: Tegucigalpa
Area: 112,492 km² (32,386 sq mi)
Population: 8,857,960
Highest Point: Cerros La Minas (2870m)
Official Languages: Spanish
GDP: $23.84 billion
Currency: Lempira
Major Religions: Christianity
Government: Presidential Republic
Geography: Tropical, Mountain
Time Zone: UTC-6
Major Cities: Tegucigalpa, San Pedro Sula

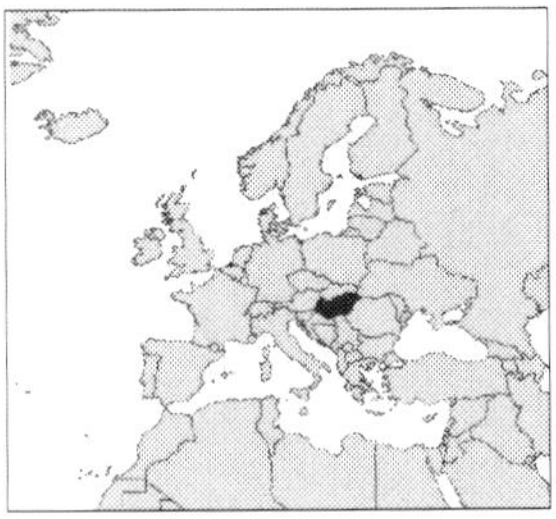

Hungary in Europe

HUNGARY

Capital City: Budapest
Area: 93,030km² (35,920 sq mi)
Population: 9,772,756
Highest Point: Kekes (1014m)
Official Languages: Hungarian
GDP: $170.40 billion
Currency: Euro
Major Religions: Christianity
Government: Unitary Parliamentary Republic
Geography: Temperate
Time Zone: UTC+1
Major Cities: Budapest, Debrecen, Szeged

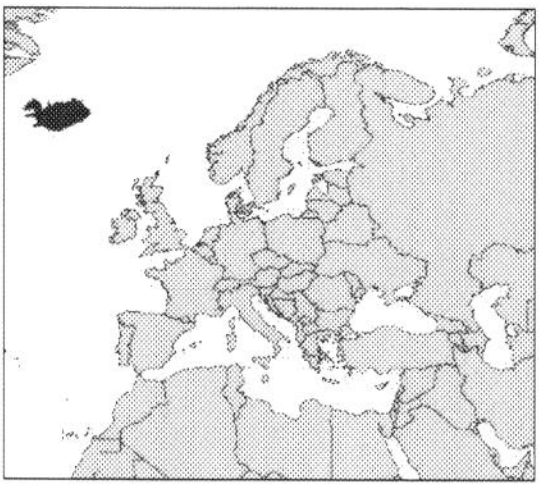

Iceland in Europe

ICELAND

Capital City: Reykjavik
Area: 102,775km² (39,682 sq mi)
Population: 358,780
Highest Point: Hvannadalshknukur (2110m)
Official Languages: Icelandic
GDP: $27.00 billion
Currency: Icelandic Krona
Major Religions: Christianity
Government: Unitary Parliamentary Republic
Geography: Tundra, Mountain, Polar
Time Zone: UTC+0
Major Cities: Reykjavik

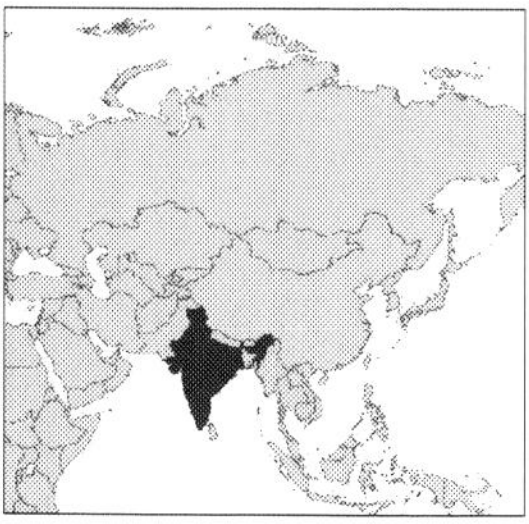

India in Asia

INDIA

Capital City: New Delhi
Area: 3,287,263 km² (1,269,219 sq mi)
Population: 1,324,171,354
Highest Point: Kangchenjunga (8586m)
Official Languages: English/Hindi
GDP: $2936.00 billion
Currency: Indian Rupee
Major Religions: Hinduism
Government: Federal Parliamentary Constitutional Republic
Geography: Tropical, Desert, Mountain
Time Zone: UTC+5:30
Major Cities: Mumbai, Delhi, Bengaluru, Hyderabad, Ahmedabad, Chennai, Kolkata

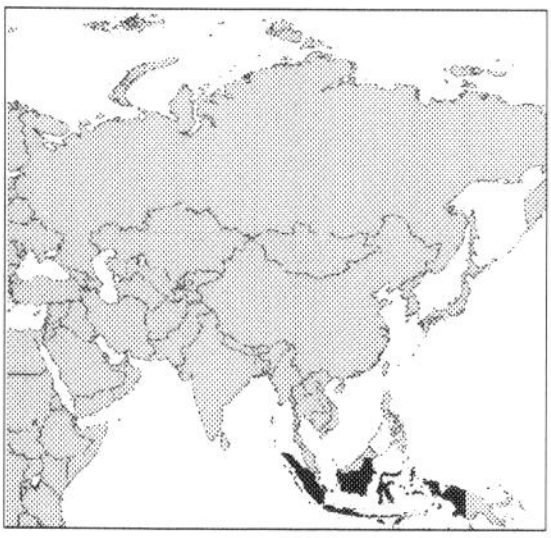

Indonesia in Asia and Australia & Oceania

INDONESIA

Capital City: Jakarta
Area: 1,904,569 km² (735,358 sq mi)
Population: 261,115,456
Highest Point: Puncak Jaya (4884m)
Official Languages: Indonesian
GDP: $1100.00 billion
Currency: Indonesian Rupiah
Major Religions: Islam
Government: Unitary Presidential Constitutional Republic
Geography: Tropical, Mountain
Time Zone: UTC+7,+8,+9
Major Cities: Jakarta, Surabaya, Bekasi, Bandung

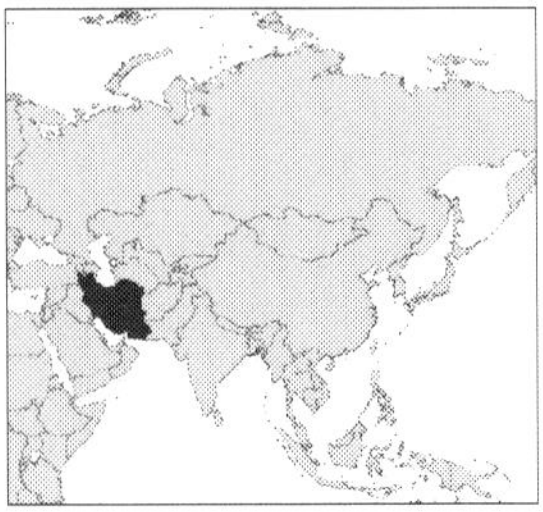

Iran in Asia

IRAN

Capital City: Tehran
Area: 1,648,195 km² (636,372 sq mi)
Population: 82,531,700
Highest Point: Mt. Davamand (5610m)
Official Languages: Persian
GDP: $484.00 billion
Currency: Rial
Major Religions: Islam
Government: Unitary Khomeist Presidential Islamic Republic
Geography: Desert, Mountain
Time Zone: UTC+3:30
Major Cities: Tehran, Mashhad, Isfahan, Karaj, Shiraz, Tabriz

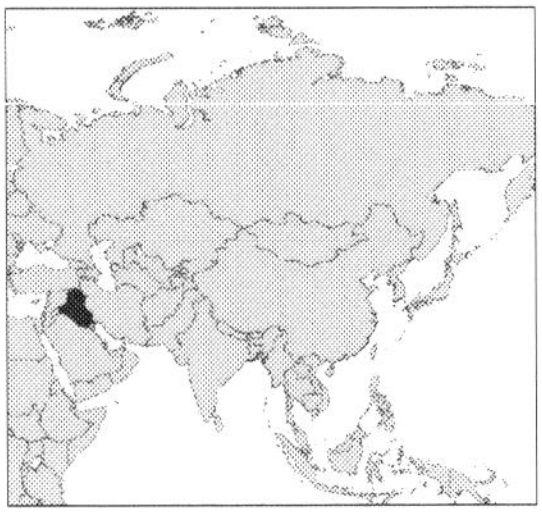

Iraq in Asia

IRAQ

Capital City: Baghdad
Area: 437,072km² (168,754 sq mi)
Population: 37,202,572
Highest Point: Cheekha Dar (3611m)
Official Languages: Arabic/Kurdish
GDP: $250.07 billion
Currency: Iraqi Dinar
Major Religions: Hinduism
Government: Federal Parliamentary Constitutional Republic
Geography: Desert
Time Zone: UTC+3
Major Cities: Baghdad, Mosul, Basra

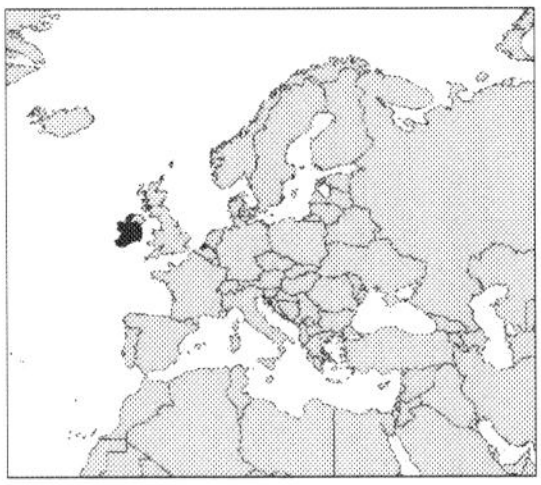

Ireland in Europe

IRELAND

Capital City: Dublin
Area: 70,723 km² (27,133 sq mi)
Population: 4,857,000
Highest Point: Carrauntoohil (1038m)
Official Languages: English/Irish
GDP: $409.00 billion
Currency: Euro
Major Religions: Christianity
Government: Unitary Parliamentary Republic
Geography: Temperate
Time Zone: UTC+7,+8,+9
Major Cities: Dublin, Cork

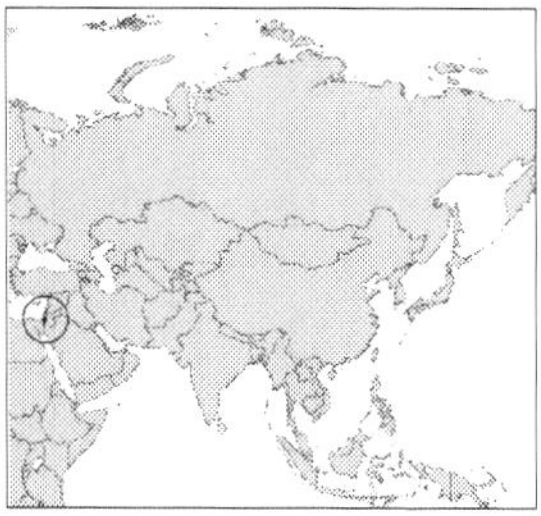

Israel in Asia

ISRAEL

Capital City: Jerusalem
Area: 20,770km² (8019 sq mi)
Population: 8,857,960
Highest Point: Mt. Meron (1208m)
Official Languages: Hebrew
GDP: $390.66 billion
Currency: New Shekel
Major Religions: Judaism
Government: Unitary Parliamentary Republic
Geography: Desert, Mediterannean
Time Zone: UTC+2
Major Cities: Jerusalem, Tel Aviv, Haifa

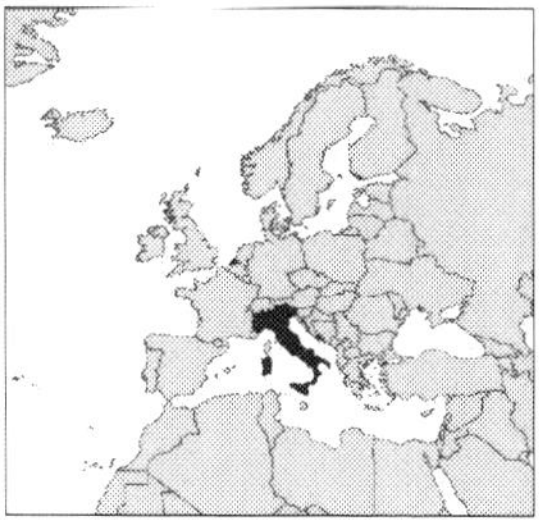

Italy in Europe

ITALY

Capital City: Rome
Area: 301,340km² (116,350 sq mi)
Population: 60,483,973
Highest Point: Mt. Blanc (4810m)
Official Languages: Italian
GDP: $1989.00 billion
Currency: Euro
Major Religions: Christianity
Government: Unitary Parliamentary Republic
Geography: Mediterannean, Temperate, Mountain
Time Zone: UTC+1
Major Cities: Rome, Milan, Naples, Turin, Palermo, Genoa, Florence, Venice

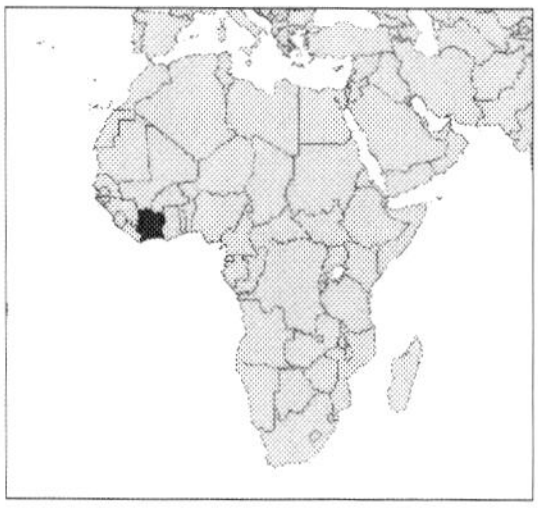

Ivory Coast in Africa

IVORY COAST (COTE D'IVORE)

Capital City: Yamoussoukro (political)
Area: 322,463 km² (124,504 sq mi)
Population: 23,740,424
Highest Point: Mont Nimba (1752m)
Official Languages: French
GDP: $48.14 billion
Currency: West African CFA Franc
Major Religions: Islam, Christianity
Government: Unitary Presidential Constitutional Republic
Geography: Savanna
Time Zone: UTC+0
Major Cities: Abidjan, Bouake

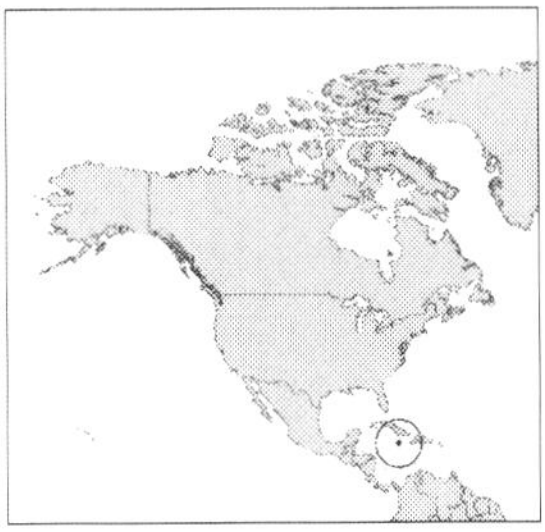

Jamaica in North America

JAMAICA

Capital City: Kingston
Area: 10,991 km² (4244 sq mi)
Population: 2,890,299
Highest Point: Blue Mountain Peak (2256m)
Official Languages: English
GDP: $15.42 billion
Currency: Jamaican Dollar
Major Religions: Christianity
Government: Unitary Parliamentary Constitutional Monarchy
Geography: Tropical
Time Zone: UTC-5
Major Cities: Kingston, Portmore, Spanish Town

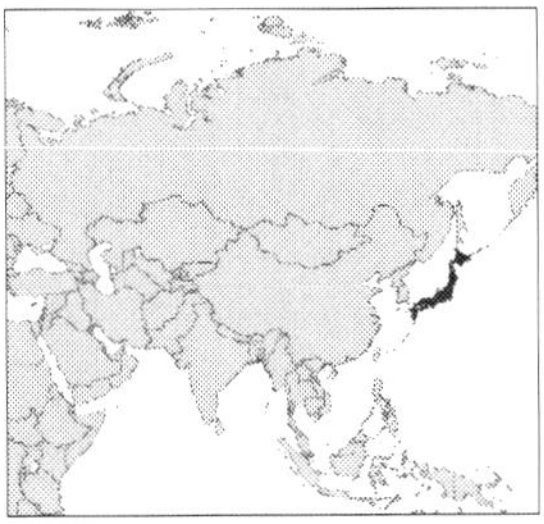

Japan in Asia

JAPAN

Capital City: Tokyo
Area: 377,973km² (145,936 sq mi)
Population: 126,440,000
Highest Point: Mt Fuji (3776m)
Official Languages: (Japanese)
GDP: $5154.00 billion
Currency: Yen
Major Religions: Irreligious, Shinto, Buddhism
Government: Unitary Parliamentary Constitutional Monarchy
Geography: Temperate, Mountain
Time Zone: UTC+9
Major Cities: Tokyo, Yokohama, Osaka, Nagoya, Sapporo

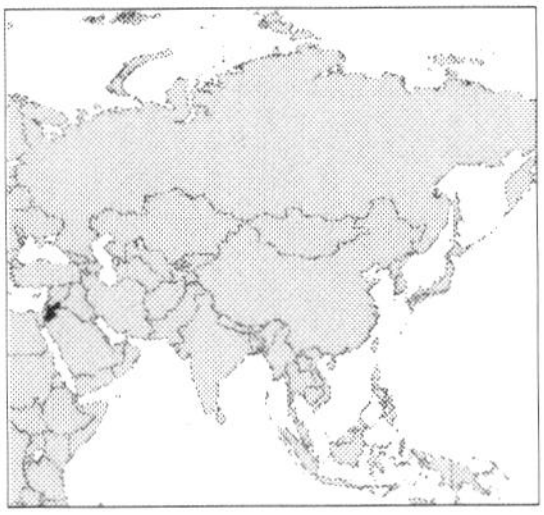

Jordan in Asia

JORDAN

Capital City: Amman
Area: 89,342km² (34,495 sq mi)
Population: 10,407,793
Highest Point: Jabal Umm ad Dami (1854m)
Official Languages: Arabic
GDP: $41.87 billion
Currency: Jordanian Dinar
Major Religions: Islam
Government: Unitary Parliamentary Constitutional Monarchy
Geography: Desert
Time Zone: UTC+2
Major Cities: Amman, Zarqa, Irbid, Russeifa

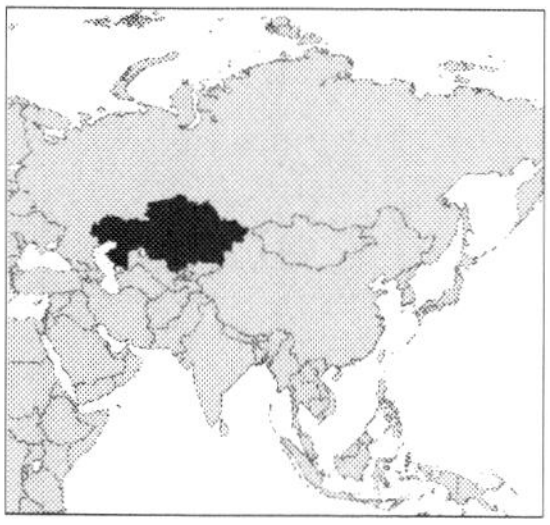

Kazakhstan in Asia

KAZAKHSTAN

Capital City: Nur-Sultan
Area: 2,724,900km² (1,052,100 sq mi)
Population: 18,448,600
Highest Point: Khan Tengri (7010m)
Official Languages: Kazakh/Russian
GDP: $164.21 billion
Currency: Tenge
Major Religions: Islam, Christianity
Government: Unitary Presidential Constitutional Republic
Geography: Temperate, Taiga, Mountain
Time Zone: UTC+5,+6
Major Cities: Almaty, Nur-Sultan, Shymkent

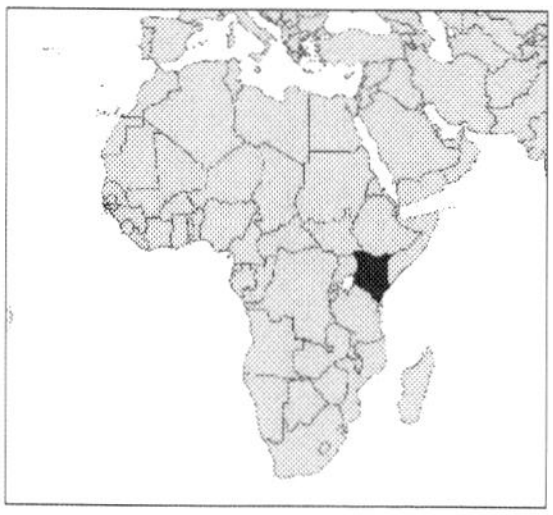

Kenya in Africa

KENYA

Capital City: Nairobi
Area: 580,367km² (224,081 sq mi)
Population: 47,564,296
Highest Point: Mt. Kenya (5199m)
Official Languages: English/Swahili
GDP: $99.25 billion
Currency: Kienyan Shilling
Major Religions: Chirstianity
Government: Unitary Presidential Constitutional Republic
Geography: Tropical, Savanna, Mountain, Desert
Time Zone: UTC+3
Major Cities: Nairobi, Mombasa, Kisumu

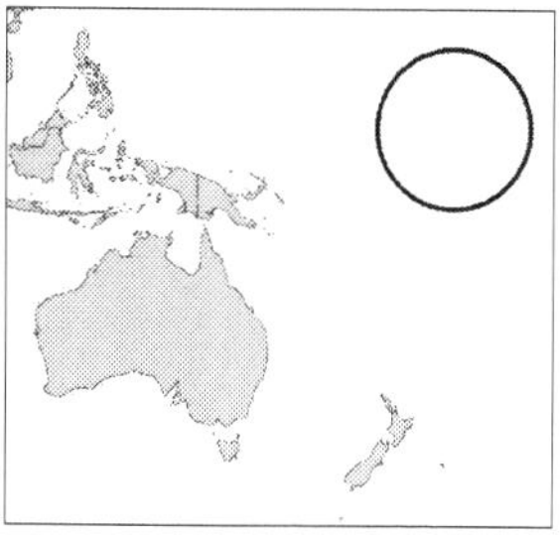

Kiribati in Australia & Oceania

KIRIBATI

Capital City: Tarawa
Area: 811km² (313 sq mi)
Population: 110,136
Highest Point: Unnamed (81m)
Official Languages: English/Gilbertese
GDP: $0.19 billion
Currency: Kiribati Dollar/Australian Dollar
Major Religions: Chirstianity
Government: Unitary Parliamentary Republic
Geography: Tropical
Time Zone: UTC+12,+13,+14
Major Cities: Tarawa

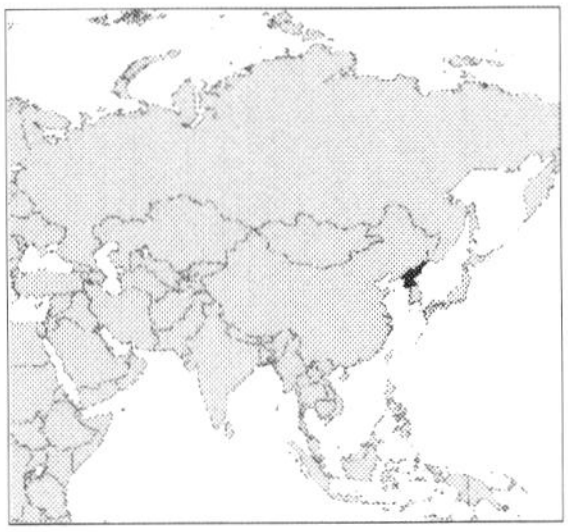

North Korea in Asia

KOREA, NORTH

Capital City: Pyongyang
Area: 120,540km² (46,540 sq mi)
Population: 25,368,620
Highest Point: Paektu-San (2744m)
Official Languages: Korean
GDP: $30.00 billion
Currency: Korean People's Won
Major Religions: Irreligious
Government: Unitary One-Party Republic
Geography: Temperate, Mountain
Time Zone: UTC+9
Major Cities: Pyongyang

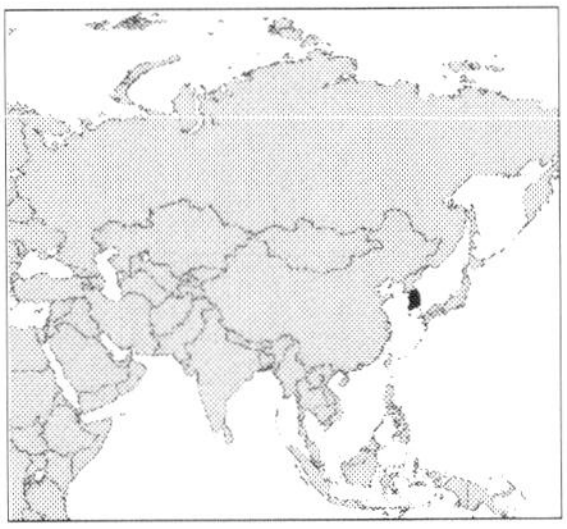

South Korea in Asia

KOREA, SOUTH

Capital City: Seoul
Area: 100,363km² (38,750 sq mi)
Population: 51,446,201
Highest Point: Halla-San (1950m)
Official Languages: Korean
GDP: $1720.00 billion
Currency: Korean Republic Won
Major Religions: Irreligious, Christianity
Government: Unitary Presidential Constitutional Republic
Geography: Temperate
Time Zone: UTC+9
Major Cities: Seoul, Busan, Incheon, Daegu

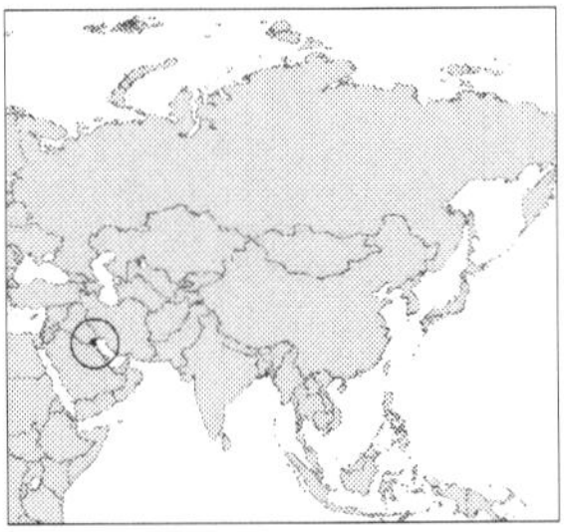

Kuwait in Asia

KUWAIT

Capital City: Kuwait City
Area: 17,818 km² (6880 sq mi)
Population: 4,621,638
Highest Point: Multa Ridge (306m)
Official Languages: Arabic
GDP: $118.27 billion
Currency: Kuwaiti Dinar
Major Religions: Islam
Government: Unitary Constitutional Monarchy
Geography: Desert
Time Zone: UTC+12,+13,+14
Major Cities: Kuwait City

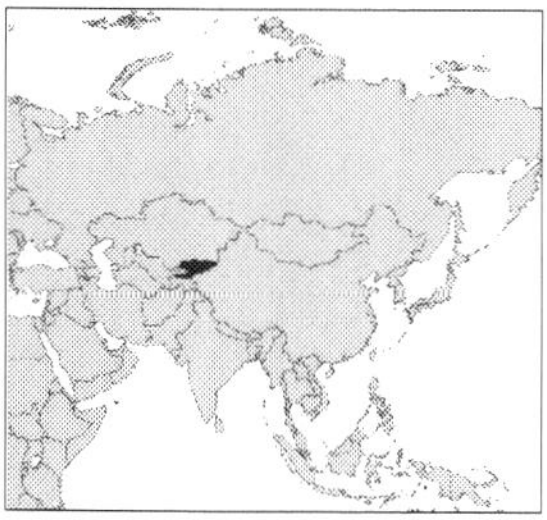

Kyrgyzstan in Asia

KYRGYZSTAN

Capital City: Bishkek
Area: 199,951km² (77,202 sq mi)
Population: 6,389,500
Highest Point: Jengish Chokusu (7439m)
Official Languages: Kyrgyz/Russian
GDP: $8.26 billion
Currency: Som
Major Religions: Islam
Government: Unitary Parliamentary Constitutional Republic
Geography: Temperate, Mountain
Time Zone: UTC+6
Major Cities: Bishkek, Osh

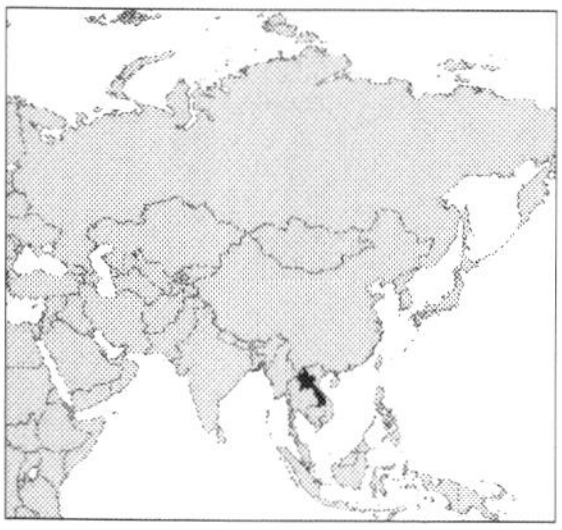

Laos in Asia

LAOS

Capital City: Vientiane
Area: 237,955km² (91,875 sq mi)
Population: 6,758,353
Highest Point: Phou Bia (2817m)
Official Languages: Lao
GDP: $20.15 billion
Currency: Kip
Major Religions: Buddhism, Tai Folk
Government: Unitary Marxist-Leninist One-Party Socialist Republic
Geography: Tropical, Mountain
Time Zone: UTC+7
Major Cities: Vientiane, Savannakhet, Pakxe

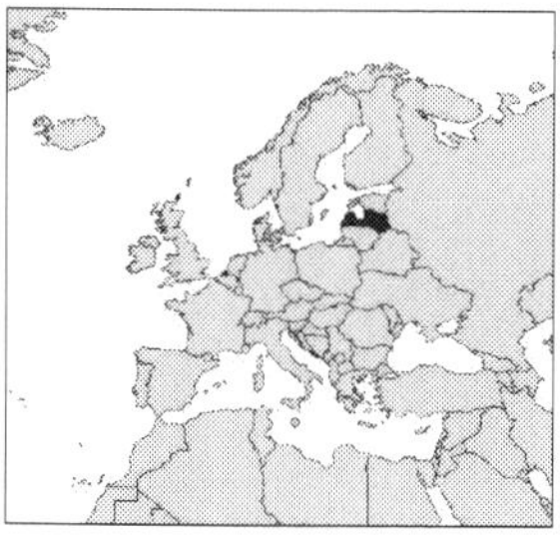

Latvia in Europe

LATVIA

Capital City: Riga
Area: 64,589km² (24,938 sq mi)
Population: 1,925,800
Highest Point: Gaizinkalns (312m)
Official Languages: Latvian
GDP: $35.72 billion
Currency: Euro
Major Religions: Christianity
Government: Unitary Parliamentary Constitutional Republic
Geography: Temperate
Time Zone: UTC+2
Major Cities: Riga

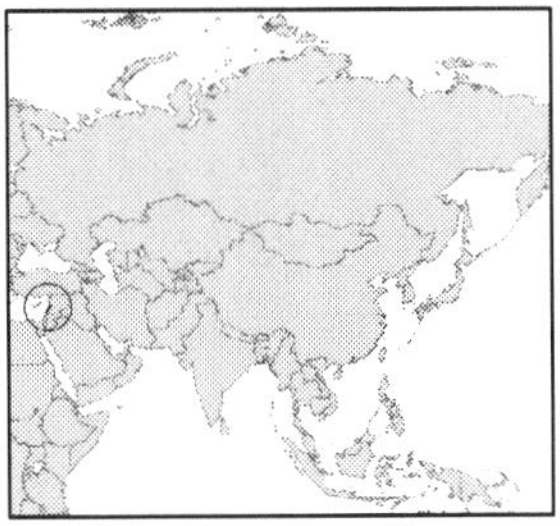

Lebanon in Asia

LEBANON

Capital City: Beirut
Area: 10,452 km^2 (4036 sq mi)
Population: 6,006,688
Highest Point: Qurnat as Sawda' (3088m)
Official Languages: Arabic
GDP: $58.00 billion
Currency: Lebanese Pound
Major Religions: Islam, Christianity
Government: Unitary Confessionalist Parliamentary Republic
Geography: Mediterranean, Mountain
Time Zone: UTC+6
Major Cities: Beirut, Tripoli

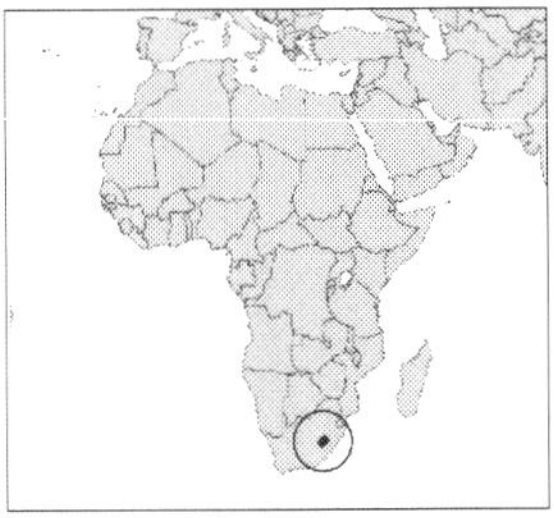

Lesotho in Africa

LESOTHO

Capital City: Maseru
Area: 30,355 km^2 (11,720 sq mi)
Population: 2,203,821
Highest Point: Thabana Ntlenyana (3482m)
Official Languages: Sesotho/English
GDP: $2.72 billion
Currency: Lesotho Loti/South African Rand
Major Religions: Christianity
Government: Unitary Parliamentary Constitutional Republic
Geography: Mountain
Time Zone: UTC+2
Major Cities: Maseru

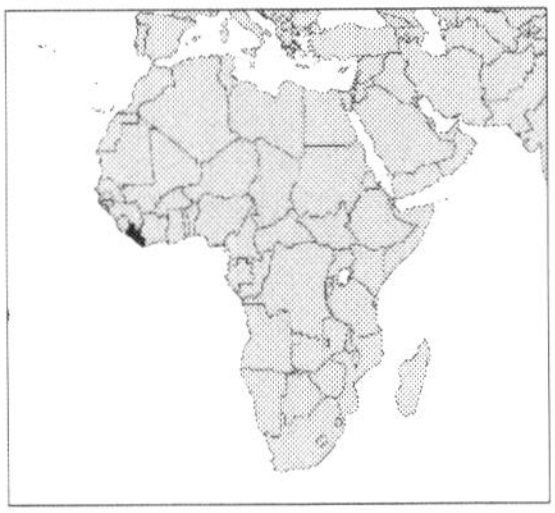

Liberia in Africa

LIBERIA

Capital City: Monrovia
Area: 111,369 km^2 (43,000 sq mi)
Population: 4,503,000
Highest Point: Mt. Wuteve (1440m)
Official Languages: English
GDP: $3.22 billion
Currency: Liberian Dollar
Major Religions: Christianity
Government: Unitary Presidential Constitutional Republic
Geography: Tropical
Time Zone: UTC+0
Major Cities: Monrovia

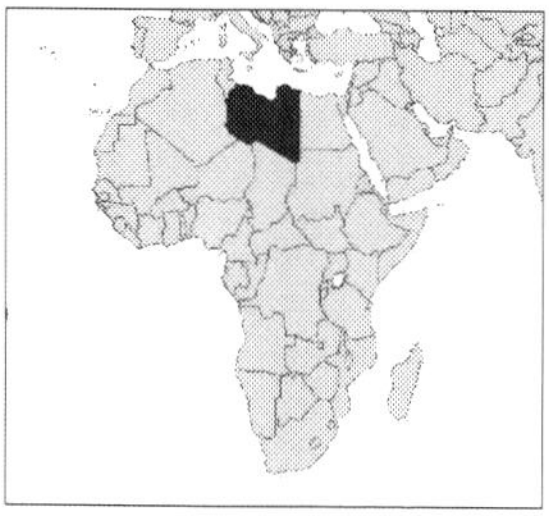

Libya in Africa

LIBYA

Capital City: Tripoli
Area: 1,759,541km² (679,363 sq mi)
Population: 6,653,210
Highest Point: Bikku Bitti (2267m)
Official Languages: Arabic
GDP: $51.33 billion
Currency: Libyan Dinar
Major Religions: Islam
Government: Unitary Provisional Government
Geography: Desert
Time Zone: UTC+2
Major Cities: Tripoli, Benghazi, Misrata, Beida

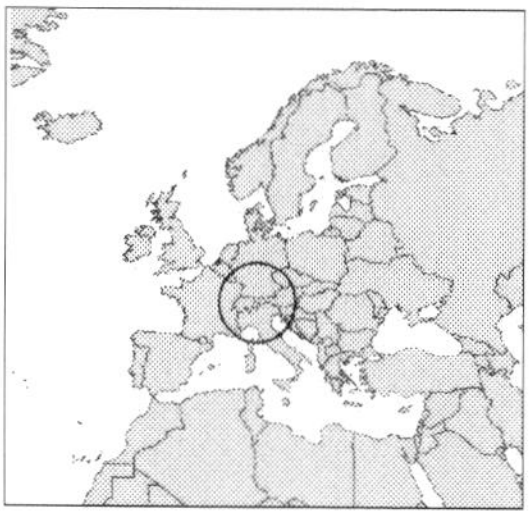

Liechtenstein in Europe

LIECHTENSTEIN

Capital City: Vaduz
Area: 160 km² (62 sq mi)
Population: 38,547
Highest Point: Grauspitz (2620m)
Official Languages: German
GDP: $5.16 billion
Currency: Swiss Franc
Major Religions: Christianity
Government: Unitary Parliamentary Constitutional Monarchy
Geography: Temperate
Time Zone: UTC+1
Major Cities: Schaan, Vaduz

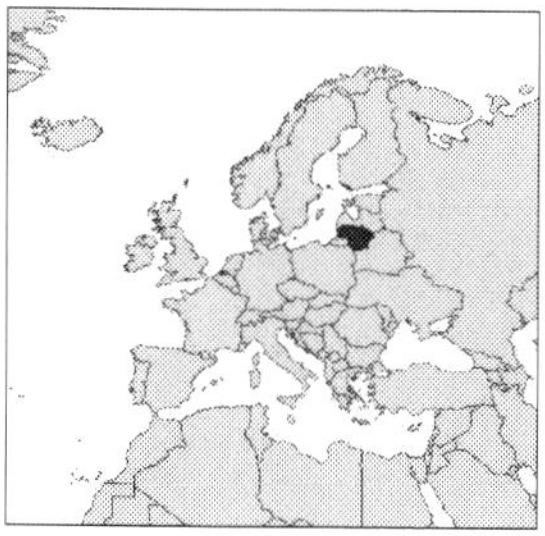

Lithuania in Europe

LITHUANIA

Capital City: Vilnius
Area: 65,300km² (25,200 sq mi)
Population: 2,791,903
Highest Point: Aukstojas Hill (294m)
Official Languages: Lithuanian
GDP: $56.00 billion
Currency: Euro
Major Religions: Christianity
Government: Unitary Presidential Republic
Geography: Temperate
Time Zone: UTC+2
Major Cities: Vilnius, Kaunas, Klaipeda

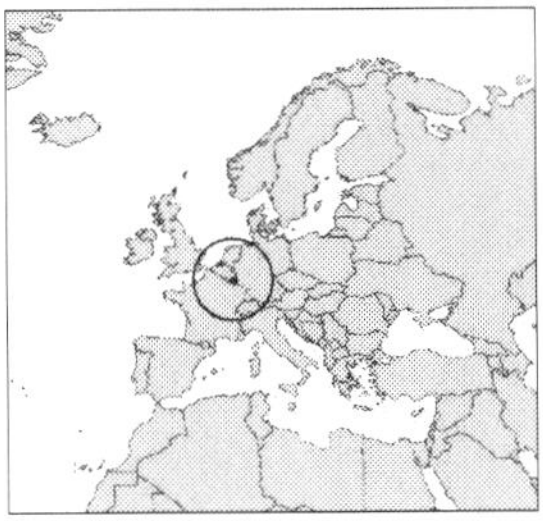

Luxembourg in Europe

LUXEMBOURG

Capital City: Luxembourg City
Area: 2586km² (999 sq mi)
Population: 602,005
Highest Point: Kneiff (560m)
Official Languages: French/German/Luxembourgish
GDP: $77.44 billion
Currency: Euro
Major Religions: Christianity
Government: Unitary Parliamentary Constitutional Monarchy
Geography: Temperate
Time Zone: UTC+1
Major Cities: Luxembourg

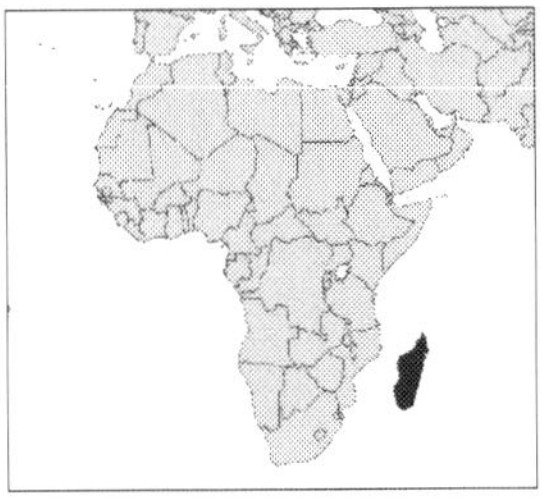

Madagascar in Africa

MADAGASCAR

Capital City: Antannarivo
Area: 587,041km² (226,658 sq mi)
Population: 24,894,551
Highest Point: Maromokotro (2876m)
Official Languages: French/Malagasy
GDP: $12.73 billion
Currency: Malagasy Ariary
Major Religions: Christianity
Government: Unitary Parliamentary Constitutional Republic
Geography: Tropical
Time Zone: UTC+3
Major Cities: Antannarivo, Toamasina, Antsirabe

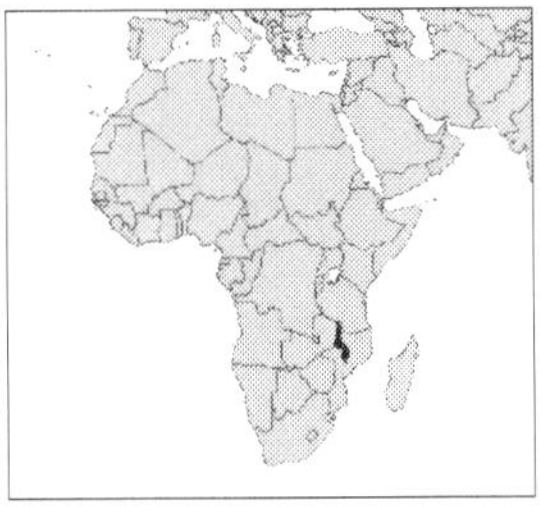

Malawi in Africa

MALAWI

Capital City: Lilongwe
Area: 118,484 km² (45,747 sq mi)
Population: 18,091,575
Highest Point: Mt. Mulanje (3002m)
Official Languages: English/Chichewa
GDP: $7.44 billion
Currency: Kwacha
Major Religions: Christianity
Government: Unitary Presidential Constitutional Republic
Geography: Mountain
Time Zone: UTC+2
Major Cities: Lilongwe, Blantyre, Mzuzu

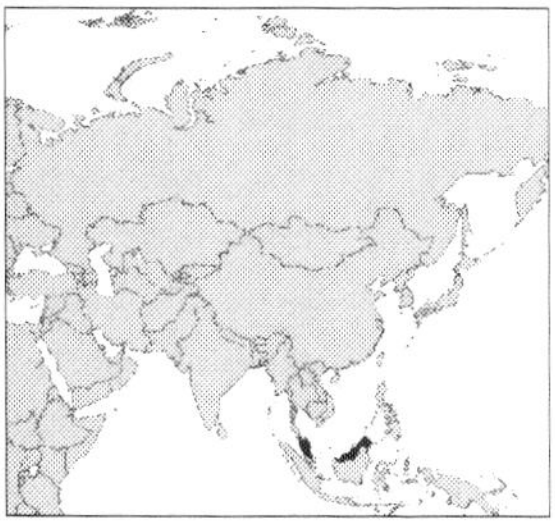

Malaysia in Asia

MALAYSIA

Capital City: Kuala Lumpur
Area: 330,803km² (127,754 sq mi)
Population: 32,049,700
Highest Point: Gunung Kinabalu (4095m)
Official Languages: Malaysian
GDP: $373.00 billion
Currency: Ringgit
Major Religions: Islam
Government: Federal Parliamentary Constitutional Monarchy
Geography: Tropical
Time Zone: UTC+8
Major Cities: Kuala Lumpur, Seberang Perai, Kajang, Klang, Subang Jaya, George Town

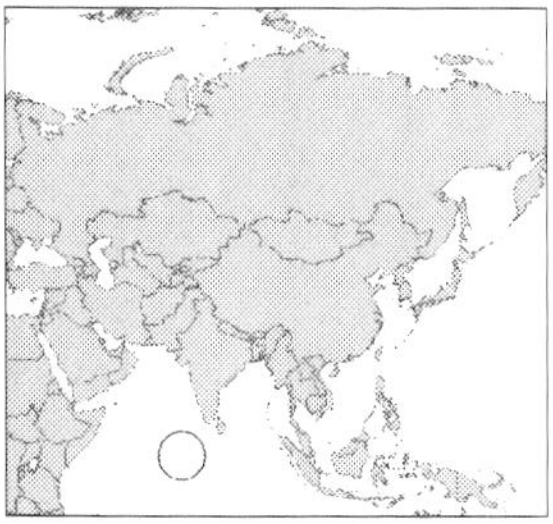

Maldives in Asia

MALDIVES

Capital City: Male
Area: 298 km² (115 sq mi)
Population: 427,756
Highest Point: Mt. Villingili (5m)
Official Languages: English/Dhivehi
GDP: $5.75 billion
Currency: Maldivian Rufiyaa
Major Religions: Islam
Government: Unitary Presidential Republic
Geography: Tropical
Time Zone: UTC+5
Major Cities: Male

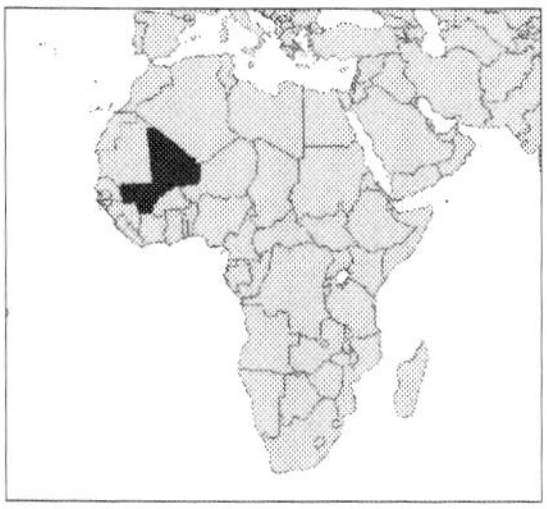

Mali in Africa

MALI

Capital City: Bamako
Area: 1,240,192 km² (478,841 sq mi)
Population: 19,329,841
Highest Point: Hombori Tondo (1155m)
Official Languages: French
GDP: $17.41 billion
Currency: West African CFA Franc
Major Religions: Islam
Government: Unitary Presidential Republic
Geography: Desert, Savanna
Time Zone: UTC+0
Major Cities: Bamako, Sikasso

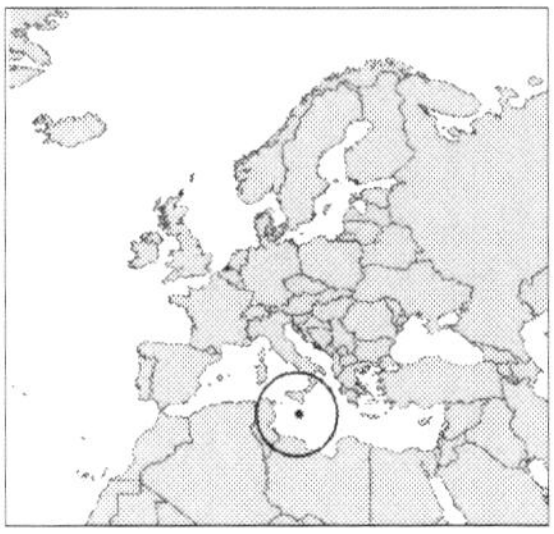

Malta in Europe

MALTA

Capital City: Valetta
Area: 316 km² (122 sq mi)
Population: 475,700
Highest Point: Ta'Dmejrek (253m)
Official Languages: English/Maltese
GDP: $15.13 billion
Currency: Euro
Major Religions: Christianity
Government: Unitary Parliamentary Constitutional Republic
Geography: Mediterranean
Time Zone: UTC+1
Major Cities: Valetta

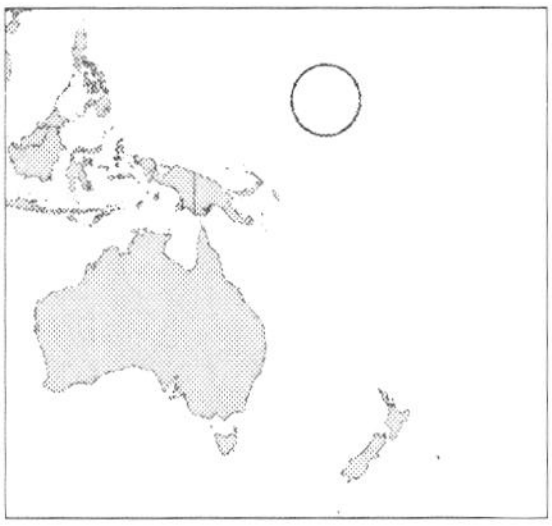

Marshall Islands in Australia & Oceania

MARSHALL ISLANDS

Capital City: Majuro
Area: 181.43km² (70.05 sq mi)
Population: 53,066
Highest Point: Unnamed (10m)
Official Languages: English/Marshallese
GDP: $0.22 billion
Currency: United States Dollar
Major Religions: Christianity
Government: Unitary Parliamentary Republic
Geography: Tropical
Time Zone: UTC+12
Major Cities: Majuro

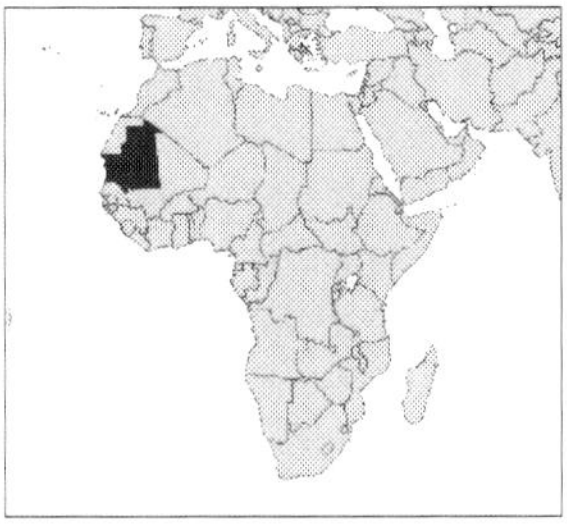

Mauritania in Africa

MAURITANIA

Capital City: Nouakchott
Area: 1,030,000km² (400,000sq mi)
Population: 4,301,018
Highest Point: Keidet et Jill (915m)
Official Languages: Arabic
GDP: $18.12 billion
Currency: Ouguiya
Major Religions: Islam
Government: Unitary Presidential Islamic Republic
Geography: Desert
Time Zone: UTC+0
Major Cities: Nouakchott, Nouadhibou

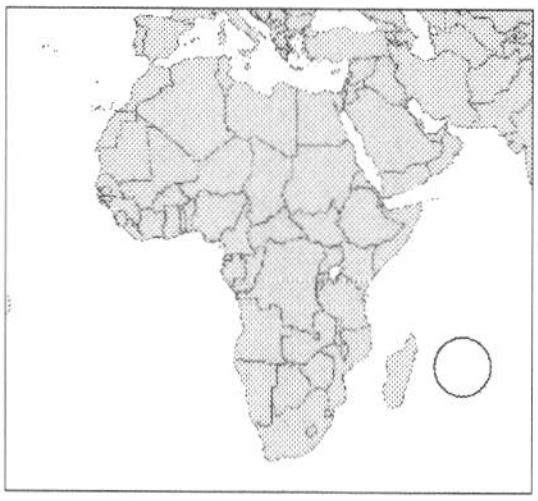

Mauritius in Africa

MAURITIUS

Capital City: Port Louis
Area: 2040km² (790 sq mi)
Population: 1,265,777
Highest Point: Piton de la Petite Riviere Noire (828m)
Official Languages: (English/French)
GDP: $14.81 billion
Currency: Mauritian Rupee
Major Religions: Hinduism, Christianity
Government: Unitary Parliamentary Republic
Geography: Tropical
Time Zone: UTC+4
Major Cities: Port Louis

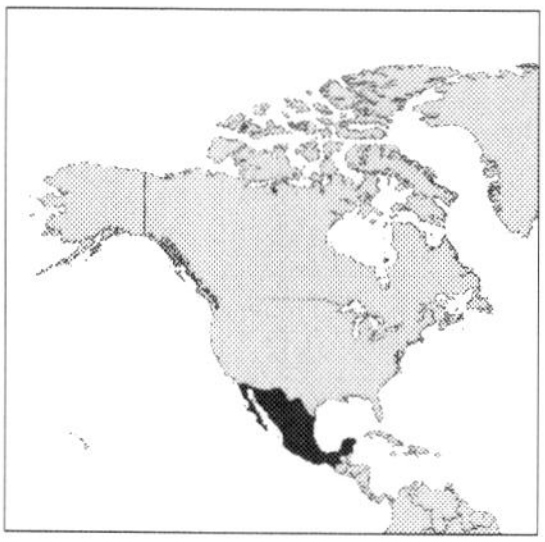

Mexico in North America

MEXICO

Capital City: Mexico City
Area: 1,972,550 km² (761,610 sq mi)
Population: 126,577,691
Highest Point: Pico De Orizaba (5636m)
Official Languages: (Spanish +68 others)
GDP: $1274.00 billion
Currency: Peso
Major Religions: Christianity
Government: Federal Parliamentary Constitutional Republic
Geography: Tropical, Desert, Mountain
Time Zone: UTC-8,-7,-6,-5
Major Cities: Mexico City, Ecatepec, Guadalajara, Puebla, Juarez, Tijuana, Leon, Monterrey

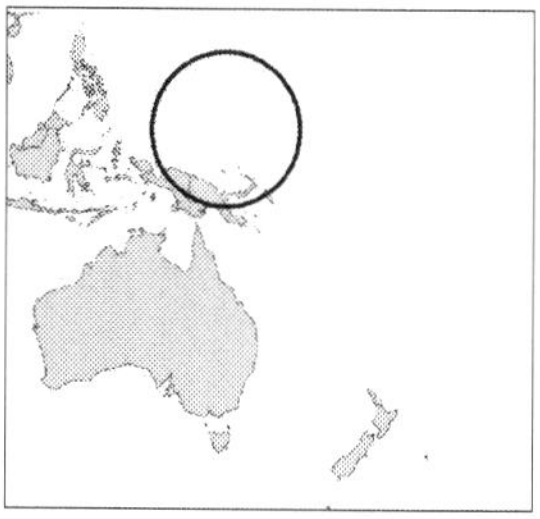

Micronesia in Australia & Oceania

MICRONESIA

Capital City: Palikir
Area: 702km² (271 sq mi)
Population: 104,937
Highest Point: Mt. Nanlaud (782m)
Official Languages: English
GDP: $0.38 billion
Currency: Ouguiya
Major Religions: Christianity
Government: Federal Parliamentary Republic
Geography: Tropical
Time Zone: UTC+10,+11
Major Cities: Weno, Palikir

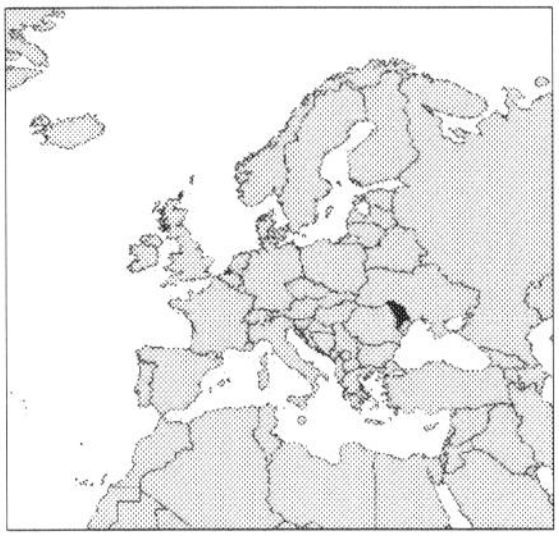

Moldova in Europe

MOLDOVA

Capital City: Chisinau
Area: 33,846km² (13,068 sq mi)
Population: 3,350,900
Highest Point: Balanesti Hill (430m)
Official Languages: Romanian
GDP: $12.04 billion
Currency: Leu
Major Religions: Christianity
Government: Unitary Parliamentary Constitutional Republic
Geography: Temperate
Time Zone: UTC+2
Major Cities: Chisinau, Tiraspol

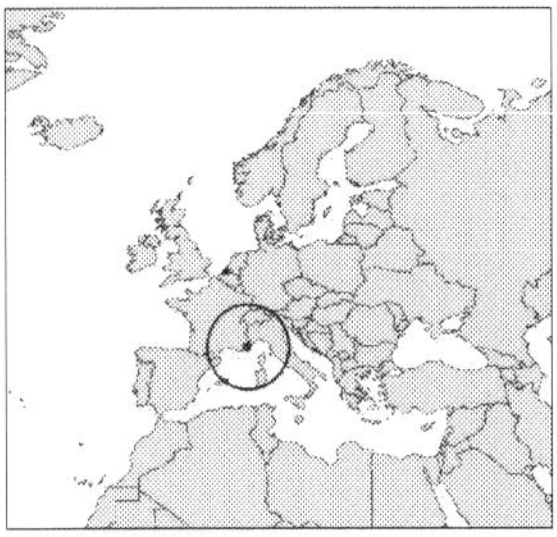

Monaco in Europe

MONACO

Capital City: Monaco
Area: 2.2km² (0.85 sq mi)
Population: 38,400
Highest Point: Unnamed (164m)
Official Languages: French
GDP: $6.40 billion
Currency: Euro
Major Religions: Christianity
Government: Unitary Parliamentary Constitutional Monarchy
Geography: Mediterranean
Time Zone: UTC+1
Major Cities: Monaco

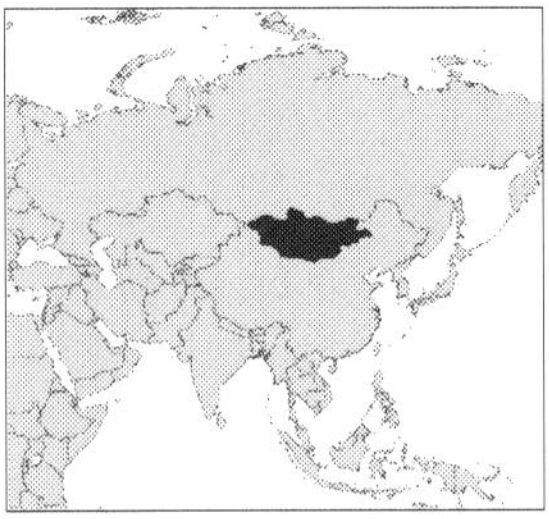

Mongolia in Asia

MONGOLIA

Capital City: Ulaanbaatar
Area: 1,566,000 km² (605,000 sq mi)
Population: 3,256,176
Highest Point: Khuiten Peak (4374m)
Official Languages: Mongolian
GDP: $13.70 billion
Currency: Togrog
Major Religions: Buddhism, Irreligious
Government: Unitary Presidential Republic
Geography: Temperate, Desert, Mountain
Time Zone: UTC+7,+8
Major Cities: Ulaanbaatar

MONTENEGRO

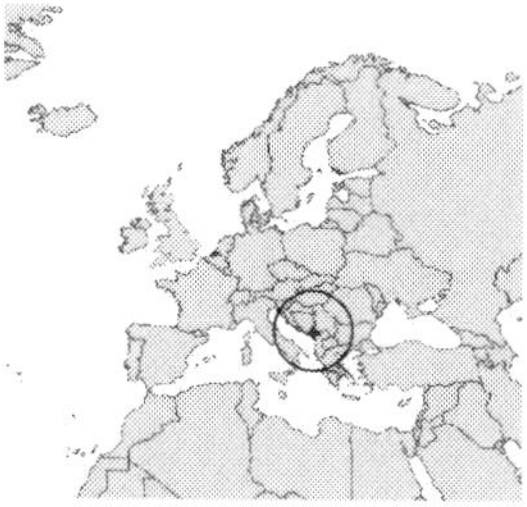

Montenegro in Europe

Capital City: Podgorica
Area: 13,812 km² (5333 sq mi)
Population: 678,901
Highest Point: Zla Kolata (2534m)
Official Languages: Montenegrin/Serbian/Bosnian/Croatian/Albanian
GDP: $5.42 billion
Currency: Euro
Major Religions: Christianity
Government: Unitary Parliamentary Constitutional Republic
Geography: Mediterranean, Mountain
Time Zone: UTC+1
Major Cities: Podgorica

MOROCCO

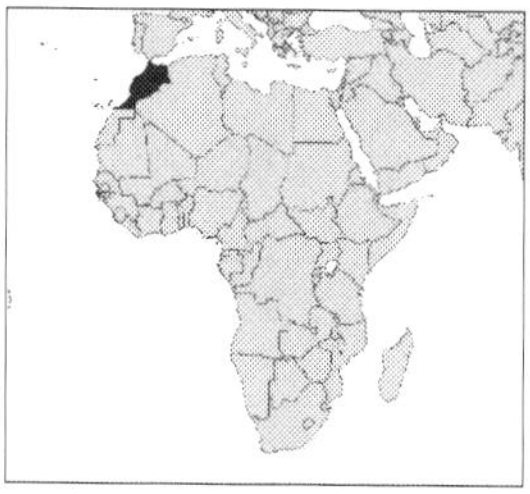

Morocco in Africa

Capital City: Al Rabat
Area: 710,850km² (274,460 sq mi)
Population: 35,740,000
Highest Point: Jbel Toubkal (4165m)
Official Languages: Arabic / Berber
GDP: $122.46 billion
Currency: Moroccan Dirham
Major Religions: Islam
Government: Unitary Parliamentary Constitutional Monarchy
Geography: Mediterranean, Desert, Mountain
Time Zone: UTC+1
Major Cities: Casablanca, Fez, Tangier, Marrakech, Sale, Meknes, Rabat

MOZAMBIQUE

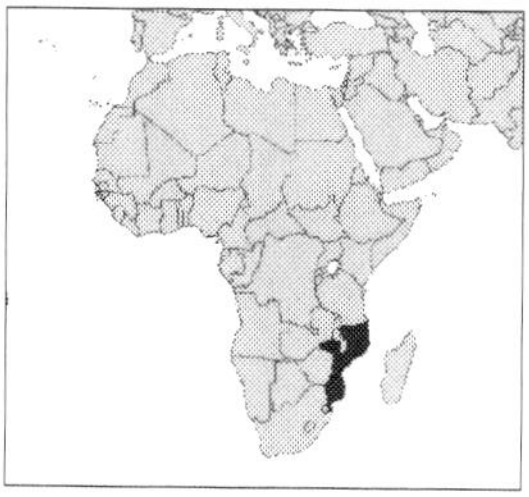

Mozambique in Africa

Capital City: Maputo
Area: 801,590 km² (309,500 sq mi)
Population: 28,829,476
Highest Point: Monte Binga (2436m)
Official Languages: Portuguese
GDP: $15.37 billion
Currency: Mozambican Metical
Major Religions: Christianity
Government: Unitary Presidential Constitutional Republic
Geography: Tropical
Time Zone: UTC+2
Major Cities: Maputo, Matola, Nampula, Beira

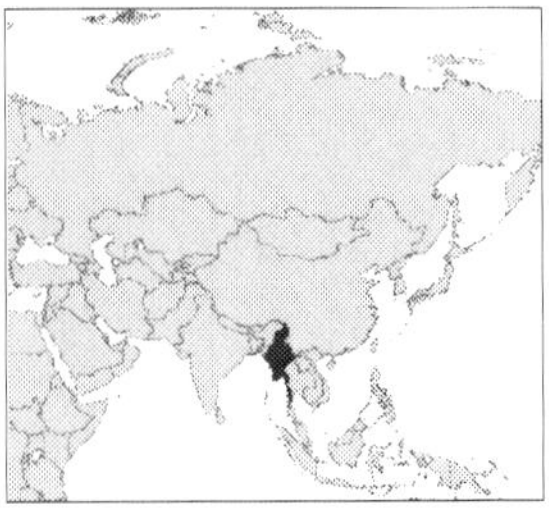

Myanmar in Asia

MYANMAR

Capital City: Naypyidaw
Area: 676,578 km² (261,228 sq mi)
Population: 53,582,855
Highest Point: Hkakabo Razi (5881m)
Official Languages: Burmese
GDP: $66.00 billion
Currency: Kyat
Major Religions: Buddhism
Government: Unitary Parliamentary Constitutional Republic
Geography: Tropical, Mountain
Time Zone: UTC+6:30
Major Cities: Yangon, Mandalay, Naypyidaw

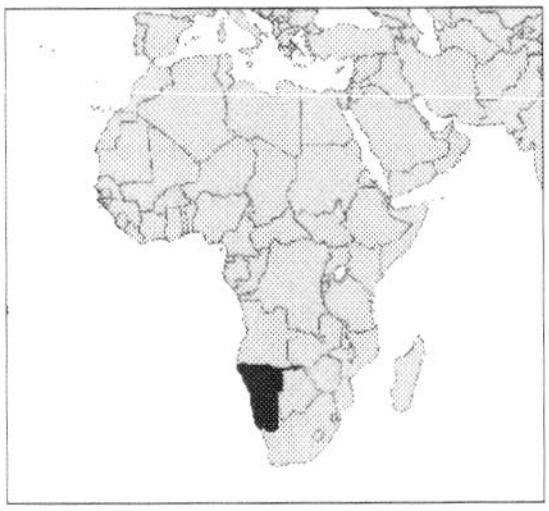

Namibia in Africa

NAMIBIA

Capital City: Windhoek
Area: 825,615km² (318,772 sq mi)
Population: 2,606,971
Highest Point: Brandberg Mountain (2573m)
Official Languages: English
GDP: $14.15 billion
Currency: Namibian Dollar, South African Rand
Major Religions: Christianity
Government: Unitary Presidential Republic
Geography: Desert
Time Zone: UTC+2
Major Cities: Windhoek

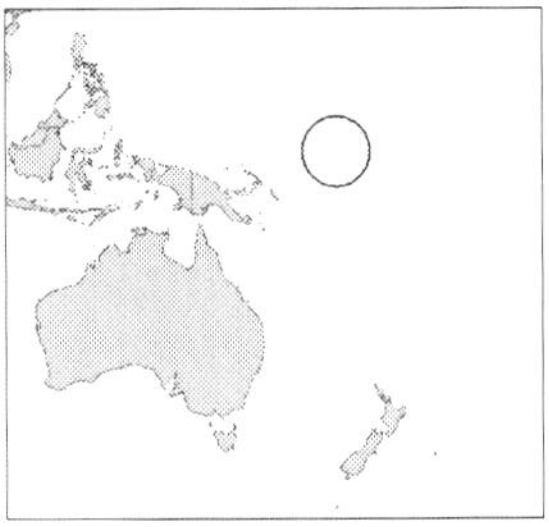

Nauru in Australia & Oceania

NAURU

Capital City: Yaren
Area: 21 km² (8.1 sq mi)
Population: 11,200
Highest Point: Command Ridge (71m)
Official Languages: Nauruan
GDP: $0.11 billion
Currency: Mozambican Metical
Major Religions: Christianity
Government: Unitary Presidential Republic
Geography: Tropical
Time Zone: UTC+12
Major Cities: Denigomodu

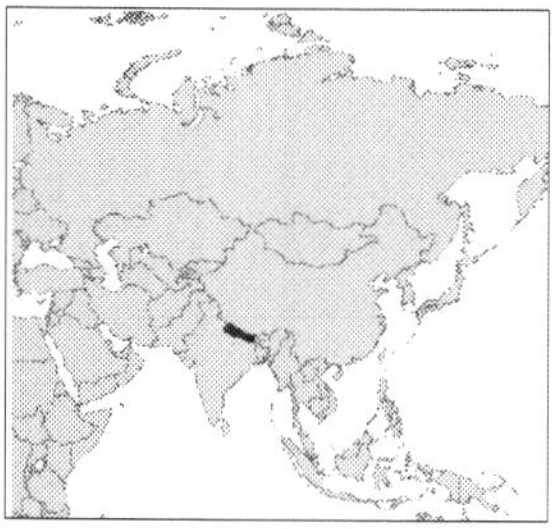

Nepal in Asia

NEPAL

Capital City: Kathmandu
Area: 147,181 km² (56,827 sq mi)
Population: 28,982,771
Highest Point: Mt. Everest (8848m)
Official Languages: Nepali/Bhojpuri/Maithili/English
GDP: $27.00 billion
Currency: Nepalese Rupee
Major Religions: Hinduism
Government: Federal Parliamentary Republic
Geography: Mountain
Time Zone: UTC+5:45
Major Cities: Kathmandu, Pokhara

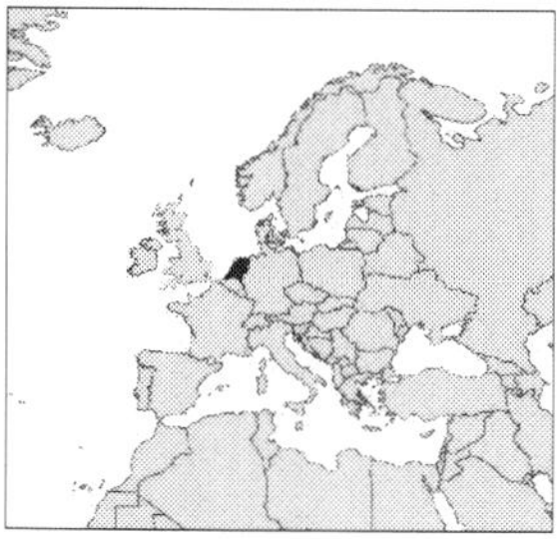

Netherlands in Europe

NETHERLANDS, THE

Capital City: Amsterdam
Area: 41,543 km² (16,040 sq mi)
Population: 17,308,133
Highest Point: Mt. Scenery (887m)
Official Languages: Dutch
GDP: $914.00 billion
Currency: Euro
Major Religions: Irreligious, Christianity
Government: Unitary Parliamentary Constitutional Monarchy
Geography: Temperate
Time Zone: UTC+1
Major Cities: Amsterdam, Rotterdam, The Hague, Ultrecht

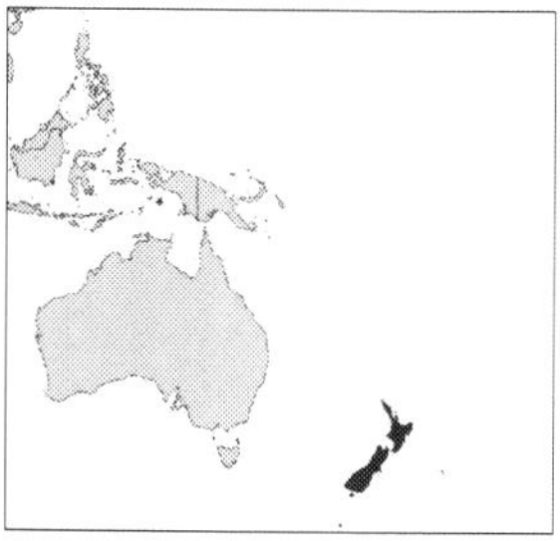

New Zealand in Australia & Oceania

NEW ZEALAND

Capital City: Wellington
Area: 268,021km² (103,483 sq mi)
Population: 4,971,640
Highest Point: Mt. Cook (3724m)
Official Languages: English/Maori
GDP: $206.00 billion
Currency: New Zealand Dollar
Major Religions: Christianity, Irreligious
Government: Unitary Parliamentary Constitutional Monarchy
Geography: Temperate, Mountain
Time Zone: UTC+12
Major Cities: Auckland, Christchurch, Wellington

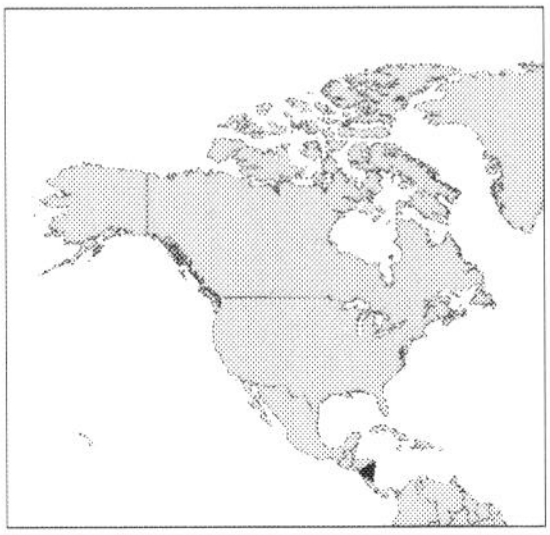

Nicaragua in North America

NICARAGUA

Capital City: Managua
Area: 130,375km² (50,338 sq mi)
Population: 6,167,237
Highest Point: Mogoton (2107m)
Official Languages: Spanish
GDP: $13.38 billion
Currency: Cordoba
Major Religions: Christianity
Government: Unitary Presidential Constitutional Republic
Geography: Tropical
Time Zone: UTC+5:45
Major Cities: Managua, Leon

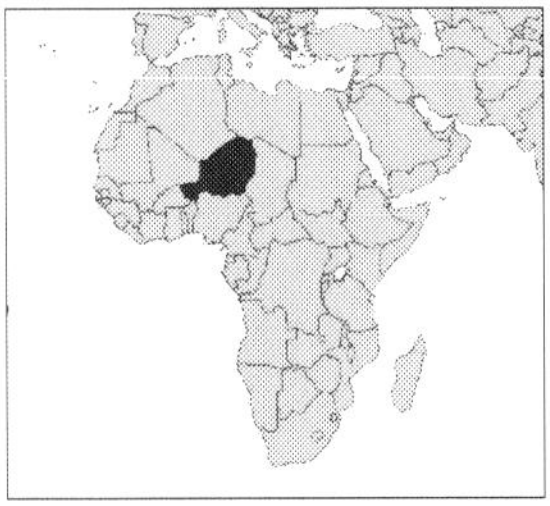

Niger in Africa

NIGER

Capital City: Niamey
Area: 1,267,000km² (489,000 sq mi)
Population: 20,672,987
Highest Point: Mont Idoukal-n-Taghes (2022m)
Official Languages: French
GDP: $9.87 billion
Currency: West African CFA Franc
Major Religions: Islam
Government: Unitary Presdiental Republic
Geography: Desert
Time Zone: UTC+1
Major Cities: Niamey, Maradi, Zinder

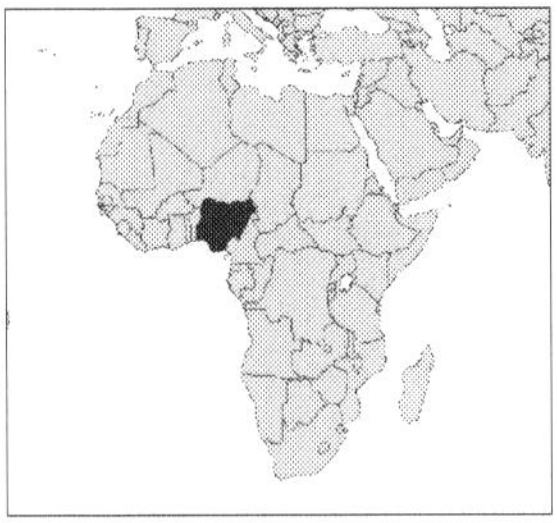

Nigeria in Africa

NIGERIA

Capital City: Abuja
Area: 923,768 km² (356,669 sq mi)
Population: 200,962,417
Highest Point: Chappal Waddi (2419m)
Official Languages: English
GDP: $447.01 billion
Currency: Naira
Major Religions: Christianity, Islam
Government: Federal Presidential Constitutional Republic
Geography: Tropical, Savanna
Time Zone: UTC+1
Major Cities: Lagos, Kano, Ibadan, Benin City, Port Harcourt

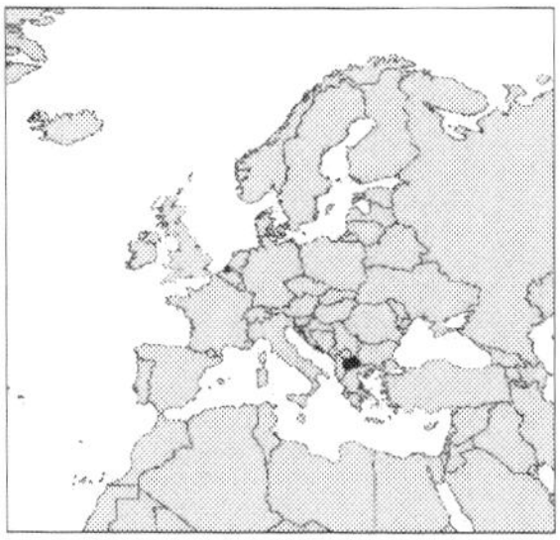

North Macedonia in Europe

NORTH MACEDONIA

Capital City: Skopje
Area: 25,713 km² (9928 sq mi)
Population: 2,103,721
Highest Point: Golem Korab (2764m)
Official Languages: Macedonian/Albanian
GDP: $12.38 billion
Currency: Macedonian Denar
Major Religions: Christianity
Government: Unitary Parliamentary Republic
Geography: Temperate, Mountain
Time Zone: UTC+1
Major Cities: Skopje

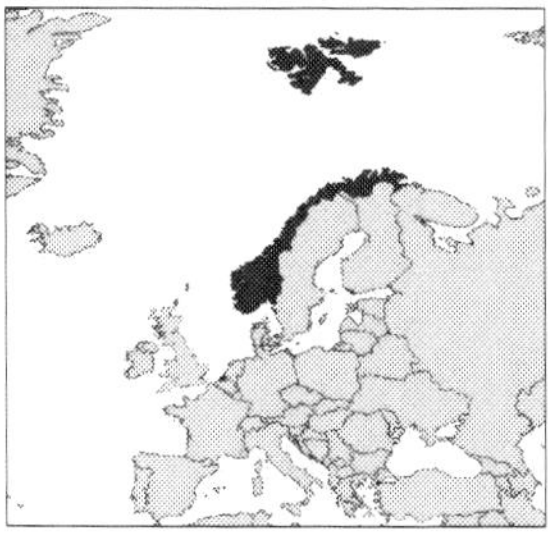

Norway in Europe

NORWAY

Capital City: Oslo
Area: 358,207 km² (148,729 sq mi)
Population: 5,328,212
Highest Point: Galdhopiggen (2469m)
Official Languages: Noweigan/Sami
GDP: $443.00 billion
Currency: Norweigan Krone
Major Religions: Christianity
Government: Unitary Parliamentary Constitutional Monarchy
Geography: Temperate, Taiga, Mountain, Tundra
Time Zone: UTC+1
Major Cities: Oslo, Bergen, Stavanger, Trondheim

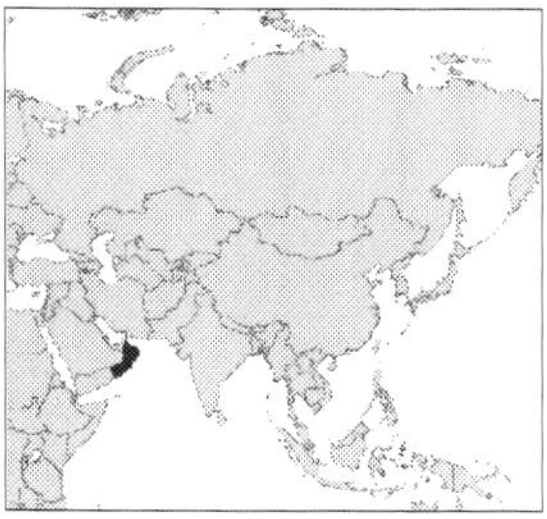

Oman in Asia

OMAN

Capital City: Muscat
Area: 309,500 km² (119,500 sq mi)
Population: 4,424,762
Highest Point: Jabal Shams (3009m)
Official Languages: Arabic
GDP: $76.61 billion
Currency: Rial
Major Religions: Islam
Government: Unitary Parliamentary Absolute Monarchy
Geography: Desert
Time Zone: UTC+4
Major Cities: Muscat, Seeb

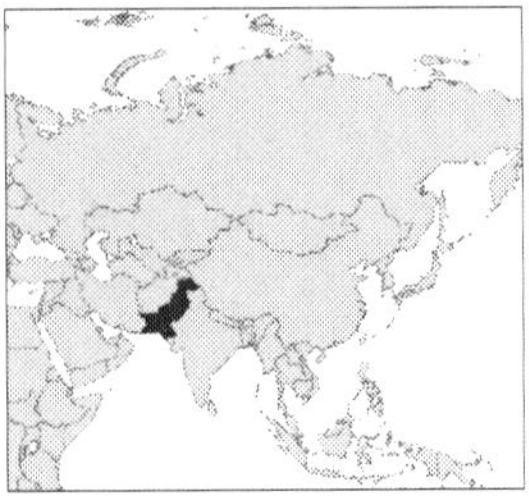

Pakistan in Asia

PAKISTAN

Capital City: Islamabad
Area: 881,913 km² (340,509 sq mi)
Population: 212,742,631
Highest Point: K2 (8611m)
Official Languages: English/Urdu
GDP: $284.20 billion
Currency: Pakistani Rupee
Major Religions: Islam
Government: Federal Parliamentary Constitutional Republic
Geography: Desert, Mountain
Time Zone: UTC+5
Major Cities: Karachi, Lahore, Faisalabad, Rawalpindi, Gujranwala

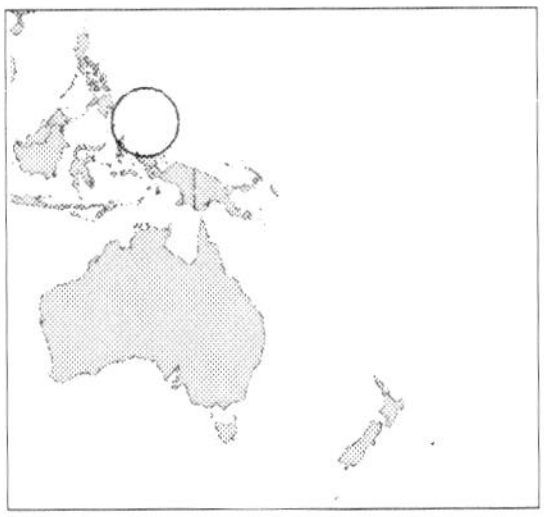

Palau in Australia & Oceania

PALAU

Capital City: Ngerulmud
Area: 459 km² (177 sq mi)
Population: 21,503
Highest Point: Mt. Ngelcherchuus (242m)
Official Languages: English/Palauan/Japanese/Sonsorolese/Tobian
GDP: $0.32 billion
Currency: United States Dollar
Major Religions: Christianity
Government: Unitary Presidential Constitutional Republic
Geography: Tropical
Time Zone: UTC+9
Major Cities: Koror

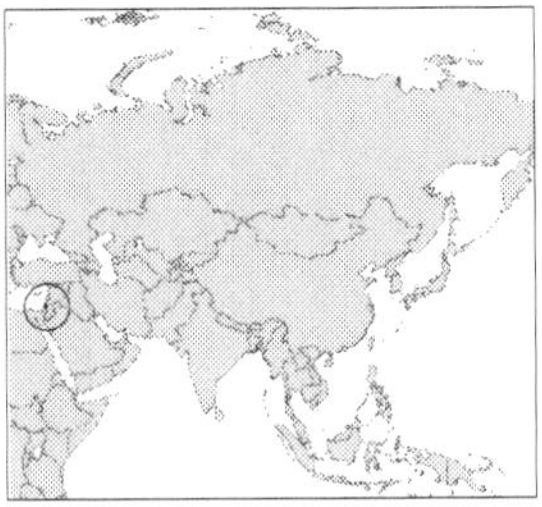

Palestine in Asia

PALESTINE

Capital City: Jerusalem
Area: 6020km² (2320 sq mi)
Population: 4,816,503
Highest Point: Mt. Nabi Yunis (1030m)
Official Languages: Arabic
GDP: $11.92 billion
Currency: Egyptian Pound, Israeli New Shekel
Major Religions: Islam
Government: Unitary Presidential Republic
Geography: Desert
Time Zone: UTC+2
Major Cities: Hebron, Gaza City, Jerusalem

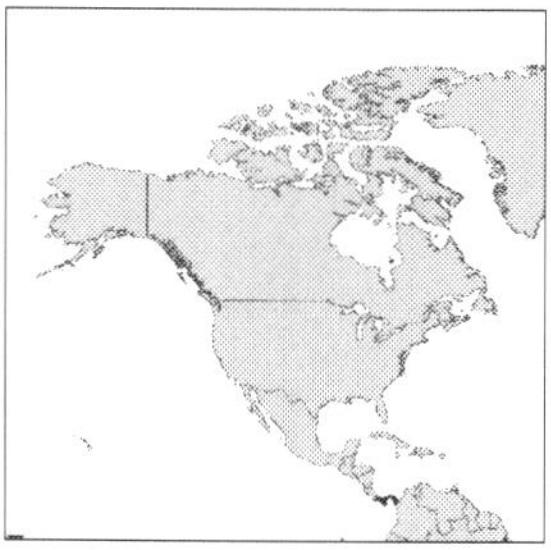

Panama in North America

PANAMA

Capital City: Panama City
Area: 75,417 km² (29,119 sq mi)
Population: 4,034,119
Highest Point: Volcan Baru (3475m)
Official Languages: Spanish
GDP: $72.22 billion
Currency: Balboa/United States Dollar
Major Religions: Christianity
Government: Unitary Presidential Constitutional Republic
Geography: Tropical, Mountain
Time Zone: UTC-5
Major Cities: Panama City, San Miguelito

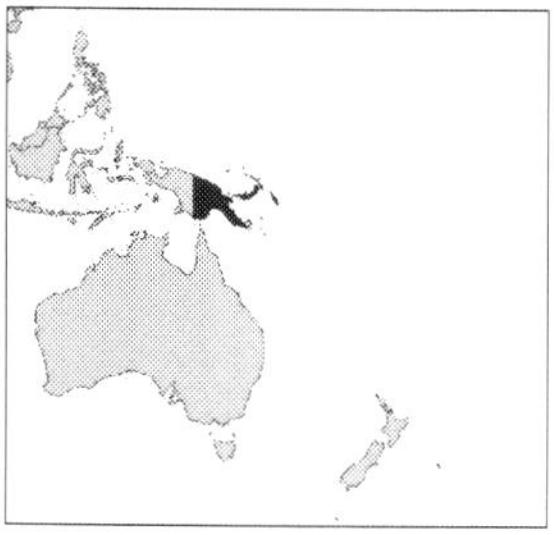

Papua New Guinea in Australia & Oceania

PAPUA NEW GUINEA

Capital City: Port Moresby
Area: 462, 840 km² (178,700 sq mi)
Population: 8,084,999
Highest Point: Mt. Wilhelm (4509m)
Official Languages: English/Hiri/Motu /Tok Pisin
GDP: $21.54 billion
Currency: Papua New Guinean Kina
Major Religions: Christianity
Government: Unitary Presidential Constitutional Monarchy
Geography: Tropical, Mountain
Time Zone: UTC+10,+11
Major Cities: Port Moresby

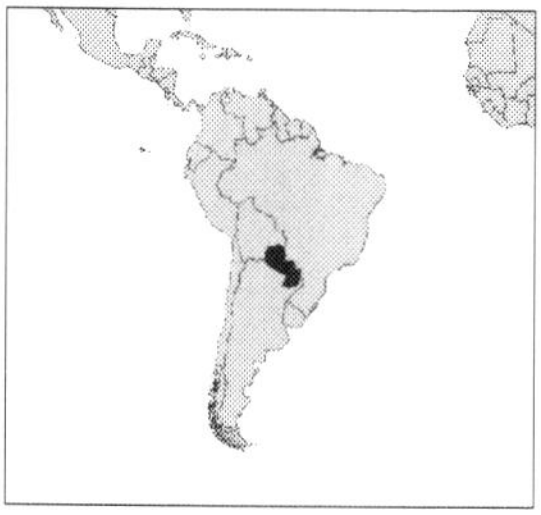

Paraguay in South America

PARAGUAY

Capital City: Asuncion
Area: 406,752 km² (157,048 sq mi)
Population: 7,152,703
Highest Point: Cerro Pero (3798m)
Official Languages: Spanish/Guarani
GDP: $44.56 billion
Currency: Guarani
Major Religions: Christianity
Government: Unitary Presidential Republic
Geography: Tropical, Savanna
Time Zone: UTC-4
Major Cities: Asuncion, Ciudad del Este, Luque

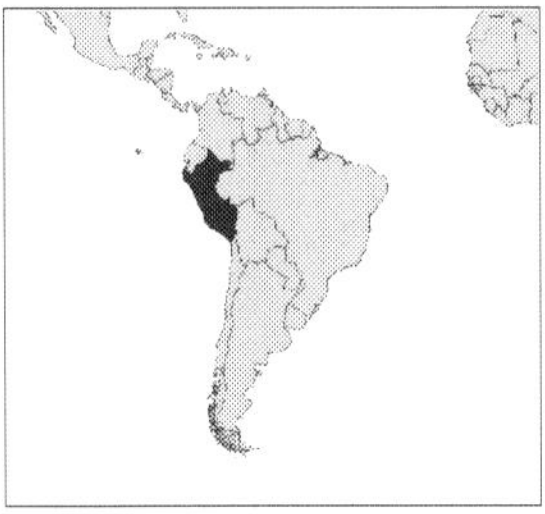

Peru in South America

PERU

Capital City: Lima
Area: 1,285,216 km² (496,225 sq mi)
Population: 32,495,510
Highest Point: Huascaran (6768m)
Official Languages: Spanish
GDP: $239.22 billion
Currency: Sol
Major Religions: Christianity
Government: Unitary Presidential Republic
Geography: Tropical, Mountain, Desert
Time Zone: UTC-5
Major Cities: Lima, Arequipa, Trujillo, Chiclayo

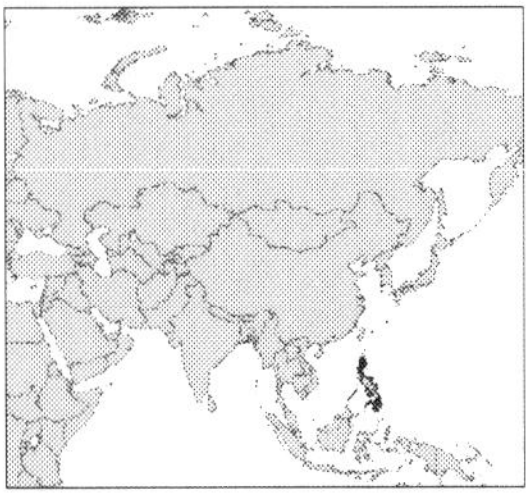

Phillipines in Asia

PHILIPPINES

Capital City: Manila
Area: 300,000km² (120,000 sq mi)
Population: 100,981,437
Highest Point: Mt. Apo (2954m)
Official Languages: Filipino/English
GDP: $383.00 billion
Currency: Papua New Guinean Kina
Major Religions: Christianity
Government: Unitary Presidential Constitutional Republic
Geography: Tropical
Time Zone: UTC+8
Major Cities: Quezon City, Manila, Davao City, Caloocan

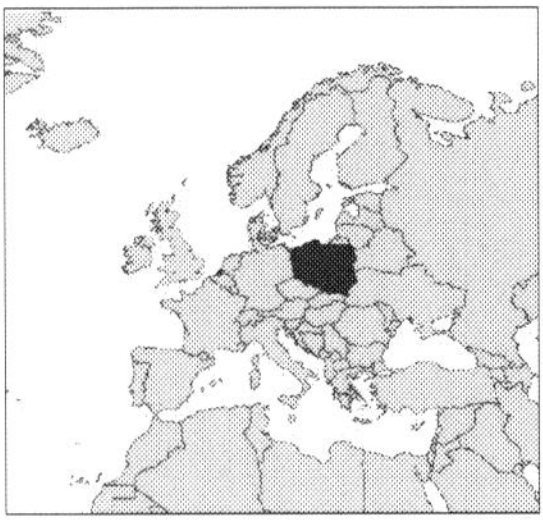

Poland in Europe

POLAND

Capital City: Warsaw
Area: 312,696 km² (120,733 sq mi)
Population: 38,433,600
Highest Point: Ryzy (2499m)
Official Languages: Polish
GDP: $607.00 billion
Currency: Polish Zloty
Major Religions: Christianity
Government: Unitary Presidential Constitutional Republic
Geography: Temperate
Time Zone: UTC+1
Major Cities: Warsaw, Krakow, Lodz, Wroclaw

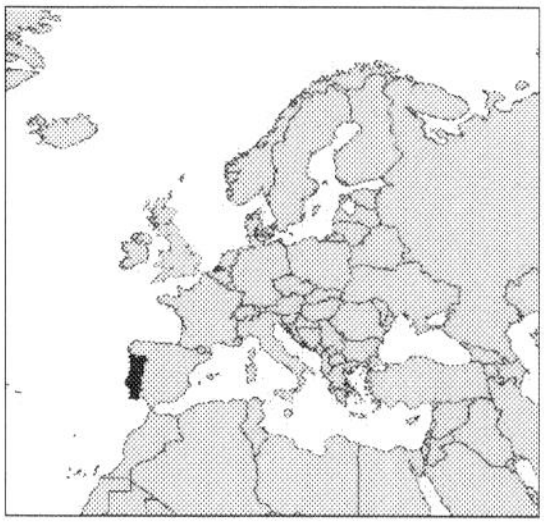

Portugal in Europe

PORTUGAL

Capital City: Lisbon
Area: 92,212 km² (35,603 sq mi)
Population: 10,276,617
Highest Point: Montanha Do Pico (2351m)
Official Languages: Portuguese
GDP: $236.41 billion
Currency: Euro
Major Religions: Christianity
Government: Unitary Presidential Constitutional Republic
Geography: Temperate, Mediterranean
Time Zone: UTC-1,+0
Major Cities: Lisbon, Porto

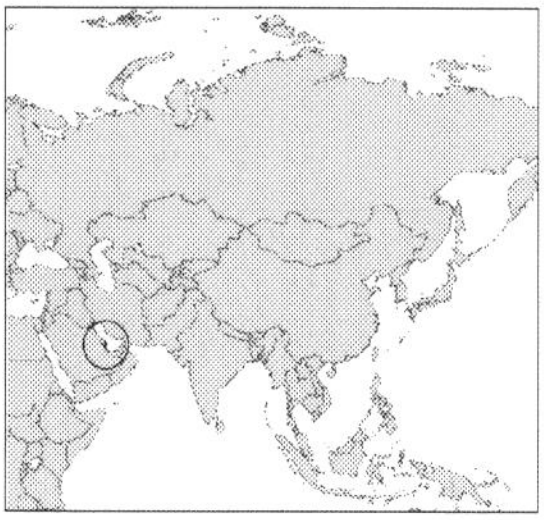

Qatar in Asia

QATAR

Capital City: Doha
Area: 11,581 km² (4471 sq mi)
Population: 2,641,669
Highest Point: Qurayn Abu al Bawl (103m)
Official Languages: Arabic
GDP: $183.81 billion
Currency: Riyal
Major Religions: Islam
Government: Hereditary Monarchy
Geography: Desert
Time Zone: UTC+3
Major Cities: Doha

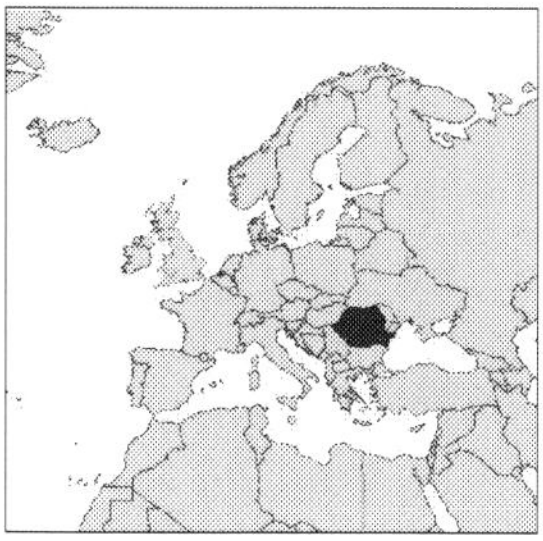

Romania in Europe

ROMANIA

Capital City: Bucharest
Area: 238,397 km² (92,046 sq mi)
Population: 19,518,117
Highest Point: Moldoveanu (2544m)
Official Languages: Romanian
GDP: $243.70 billion
Currency: Romanian Leu
Major Religions: Christianity
Government: Unitary Presidential Republic
Geography: Temperate
Time Zone: UTC+2
Major Cities: Bucharest, Cluj-Napoca, Timisoara, Iasi, Constanta

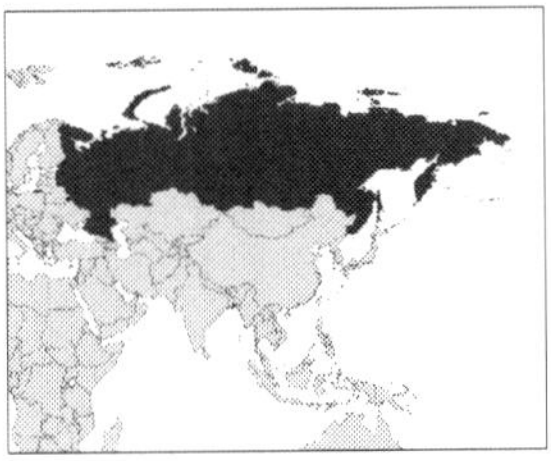

Russia in Europe and Asia

RUSSIA

Capital City: Moscow
Area: 17,098,246 km² (6,601,670 sq mi)
Population: 146,793,744
Highest Point: Mt. Elbrus (5642m)
Official Languages: Russian
GDP: $1638.00 billion
Currency: Russian Ruble
Major Religions: Christianity
Government: Federal Presidential Constitutional Republic
Geography: Temperate, Taiga, Tundra, Polar
Time Zone: UTC+2 to +12
Major Cities: Moscow, St. Petersburg, Novosibirsk, Yekaterinburg

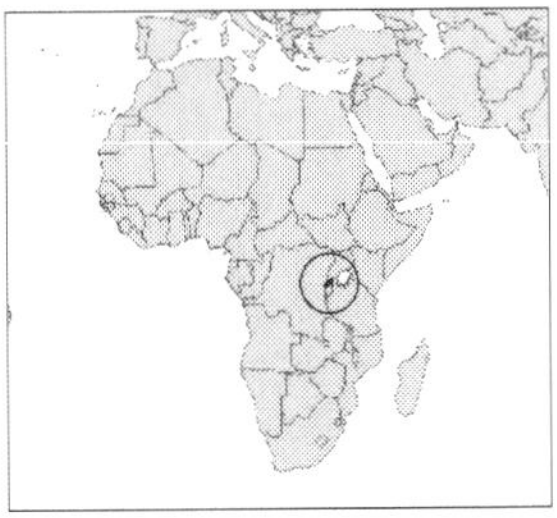

Rwanda in Africa

RWANDA

Capital City: Kigali
Area: 26,338 km² (10,169 sq mi)
Population: 11,262,564
Highest Point: Mt. Karisimbi (4507m)
Official Languages: English/French/Swahili/Kinyarwanda
GDP: $10.21 billion
Currency: Rwandan Franc
Major Religions: Christianity
Government: Unitary Presidential Constitutional Republic
Geography: Mountain
Time Zone: UTC+2
Major Cities: Kigali

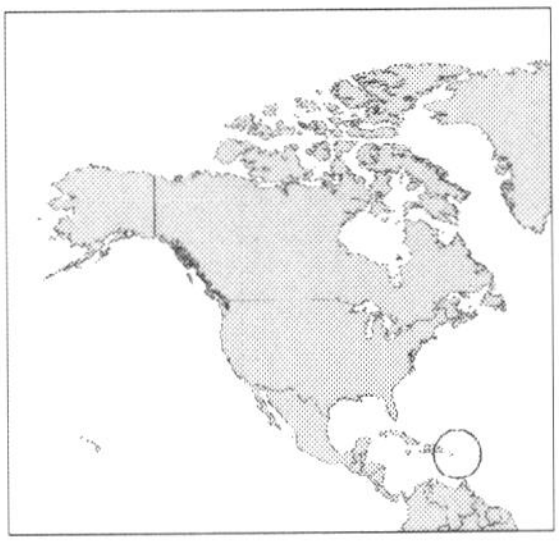

Saint Kitts and Nevis in North America

SAINT KITTS AND NEVIS

Capital City: Basseterre
Area: 261km² (101 sq mi)
Population: 54,821
Highest Point: Mt. Liamuiga (1156m)
Official Languages: English
GDP: $1.06 billion
Currency: East Caribbean Dollar
Major Religions: Christianity
Government: Federal Parliamentary Constitutional Monarchy
Geography: Tropical
Time Zone: UTC-4
Major Cities: Bassaterre

Saint Lucia in North America

SAINT LUCIA

Capital City: Castries
Area: 617km² (238 sq mi)
Population: 178,015
Highest Point: Mt. Gimie (950m)
Official Languages: English
GDP: $1.77 billion
Currency: East Caribbean Dollar
Major Religions: Christianity
Government: Unitary Parliamentary Constitutional Monarchy
Geography: Tropical
Time Zone: UTC-4
Major Cities: Castries

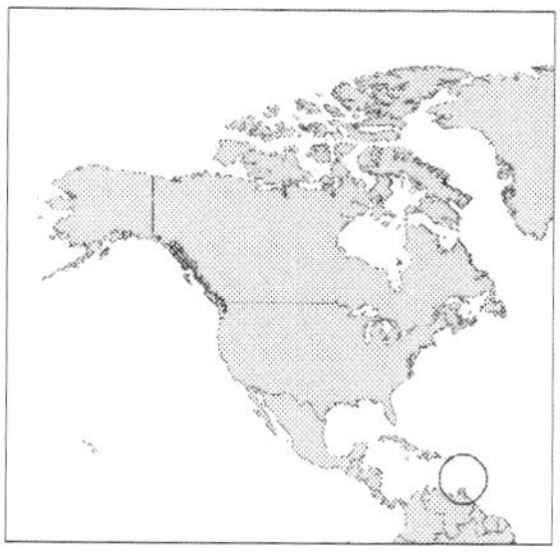
Saint Vincent and The Grenadines in North America

SAINT VINCENT AND THE GRENADINES

Capital City: Kingstown
Area: 389 km² (150 sq mi)
Population: 109,643
Highest Point: La Soufriere (1234m)
Official Languages: English
GDP: $0.86 billion
Currency: East Caribbean Dollar
Major Religions: Christianity
Government: Unitary Presidential Constitutional Monarchy
Geography: Tropical
Time Zone: UTC-4
Major Cities: Kingstown

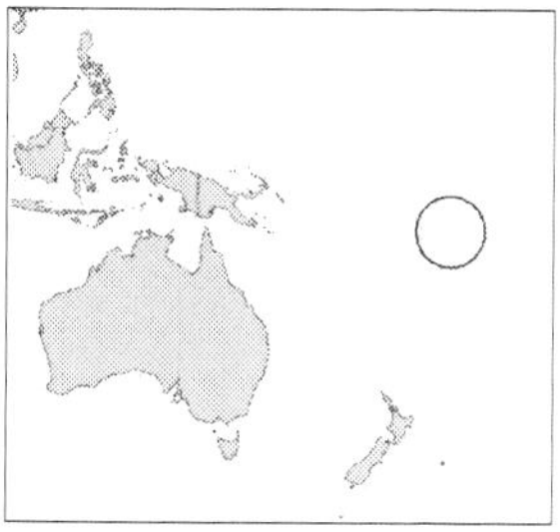
Samoa in Australia & Oceania

SAMOA

Capital City: Apia
Area: 2842km² (1097 sq mi)
Population: 195,843
Highest Point: Mauga Silisili (1857m)
Official Languages: English/Samoan
GDP: $0.88 billion
Currency: Tala
Major Religions: Christianity
Government: Unitary Parliamentary Democracy under elective Monarchy
Geography: Tropical
Time Zone: UTC+13
Major Cities: Apia

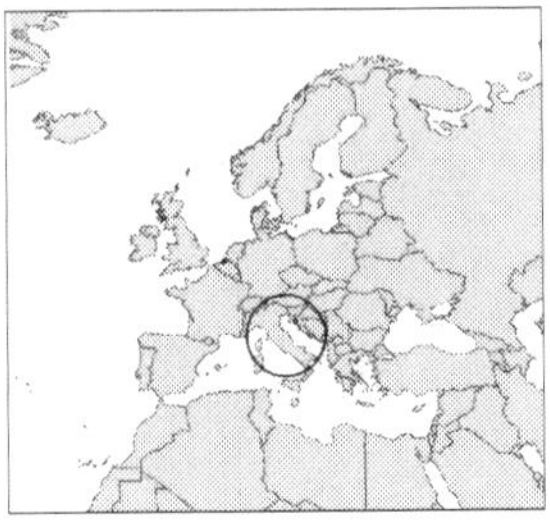

San Marino in Europe

SAN MARINO

Capital City: San Marino
Area: 61km² (24 sq mi)
Population: 33,344
Highest Point: Monte Titano (739m)
Official Languages: Italian
GDP: $1.55 billion
Currency: Euro
Major Religions: Christianity
Government: Unitary Parliamentary Diarchic Directorial Republic
Geography: Temperate
Time Zone: UTC+1
Major Cities: Dogana, San Marino

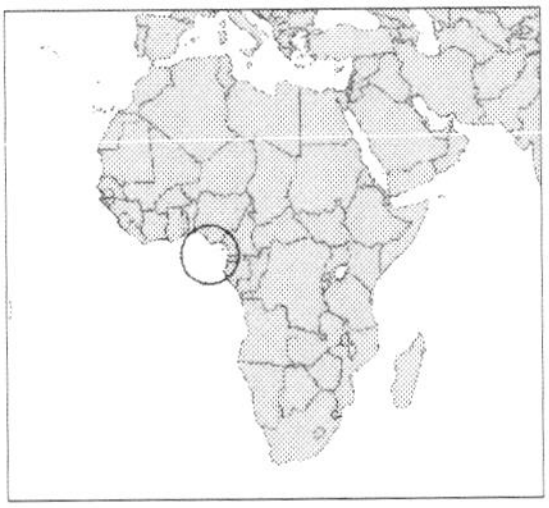

Sao Tome & Principe in Africa

SAO TOME AND PRINCIPE

Capital City: Sao Tome
Area: 1001km² (386 sq mi)
Population: 199,910
Highest Point: Pico de Sao Tome (2024m)
Official Languages: Portuguese
GDP: $0.36 billion
Currency: Dobra
Major Religions: Christianity
Government: Unitary Presidential Republic
Geography: Tropical
Time Zone: UTC+0
Major Cities: Sao Tome

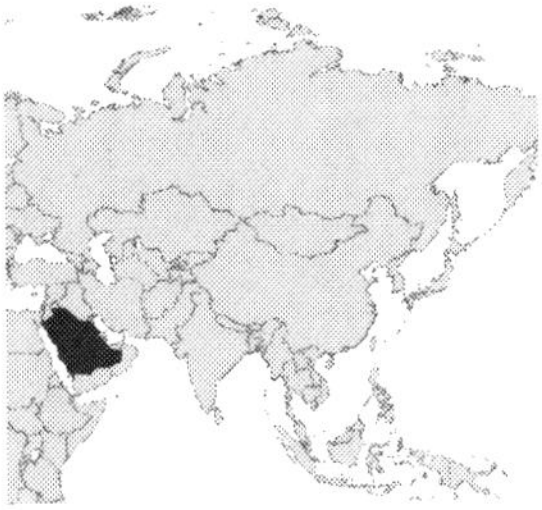

Saudi Arabia in Asia

SAUDI ARABIA

Capital City: Riyadh
Area: 2,149,690 km² (830,000 sq mi)
Population: 33,000,000
Highest Point: Jabal Sawda (3000m)
Official Languages: Arabic
GDP: $779.29 billion
Currency: Saudi Riyal
Major Religions: Islam
Government: Unitary Islamic Absolute Monarchy under Dictatorship
Geography: Desert
Time Zone: UTC+3
Major Cities: Riyadh, Jeddah, Mecca, Medina

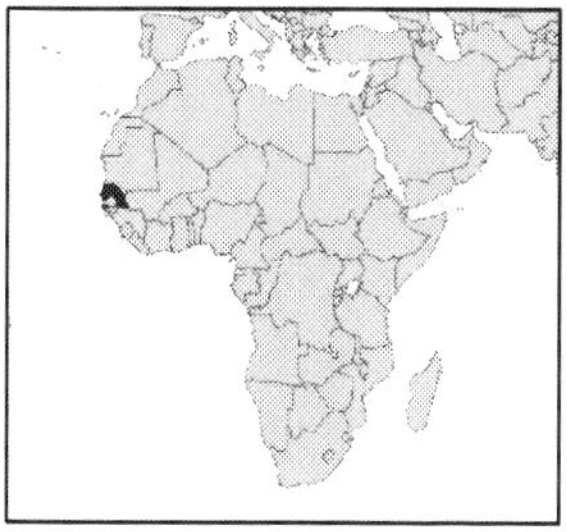

Senegal in Africa

SENEGAL

Capital City: Dakar
Area: 196,712 km^2 (75,951 sq mi)
Population: 15,411,614
Highest Point: Unnamed (648m)
Official Languages: French
GDP: $24.24 billion
Currency: West African CFA Franc
Major Religions: Islam
Government: Unitary Presidential Republic
Geography: Savanna, Desert
Time Zone: UTC+0
Major Cities: Dakar, Touba, Thies

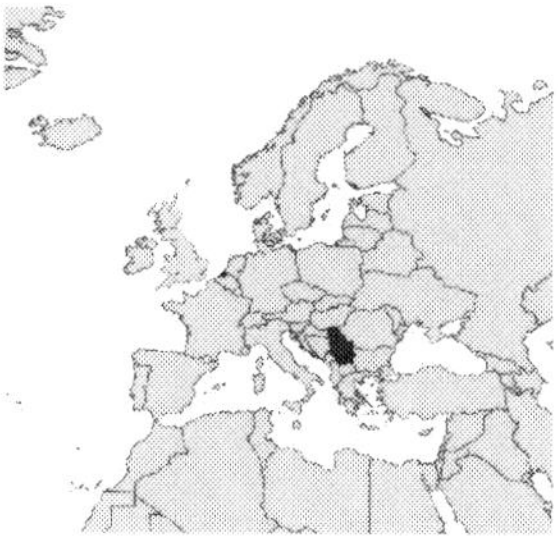

Serbia in Europe

SERBIA

Capital City: Belgrade
Area: 88,361km^2 (34,116 sq mi)
Population: 6,963,764
Highest Point: Midzor (2169m)
Official Languages: Serbian
GDP: $56.89 billion
Currency: Serbian Dinar
Major Religions: Christianity
Government: Unitary Parliamentary Constitutional Republic
Geography: Temperate
Time Zone: UTC+1
Major Cities: Belgrade, Novi Sad

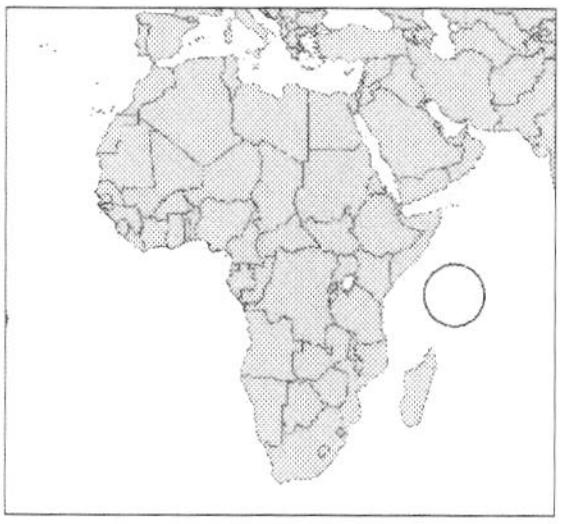

Seychelles in Africa

SEYCHELLES

Capital City: Victoria
Area: 459km^2 (177 sq mi)
Population: 94,228
Highest Point: Morne Seychellois (905m)
Official Languages: English/French/ Seychellois Creole
GDP: $1.56 billion
Currency: Seychellois Rupee
Major Religions: Christianity
Government: Unitary Presidential Republic
Geography: Tropical
Time Zone: UTC+4
Major Cities: Victoria

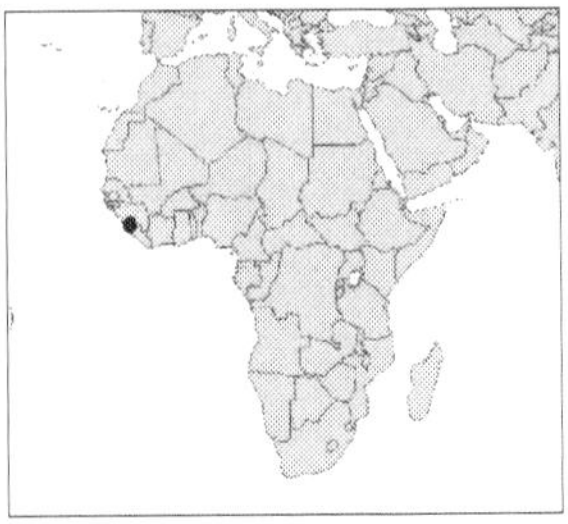

Sierra Leone in Africa

SIERRA LEONE

Capital City: Freetown
Area: 71,740 km² (27,700 sq mi)
Population: 7,075,641
Highest Point: Mt. Bintumani (1948m)
Official Languages: English
GDP: $3.82 billion
Currency: Leone
Major Religions: Islam
Government: Unitary Presidential Constitutional Republic
Geography: Savanna, Tropical
Time Zone: UTC+0
Major Cities: Freetown, Kenema, Bo

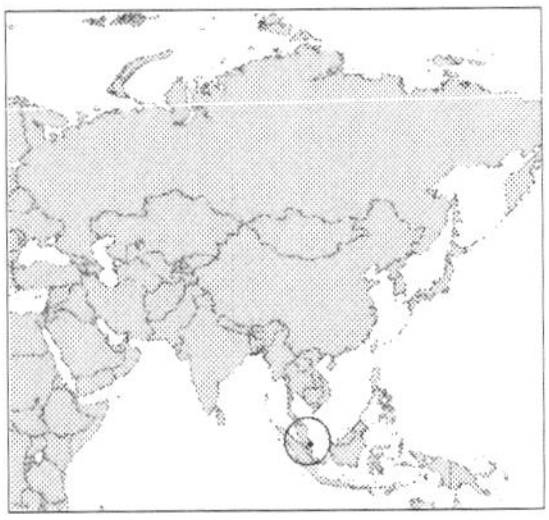

Singapore in Asia

SINGAPORE

Capital City: Singapore
Area: 723km² (279 sq mi)
Population: 5,638,700
Highest Point: Bukit Timah Hill (164m)
Official Languages: English/Malay/Chinese /Tamil
GDP: $372.81 billion
Currency: Singapore Dollar
Major Religions: Buddhism
Government: Unitary Parliamentary Constitutional Republic
Geography: Tropical
Time Zone: UTC+8
Major Cities: Singapore

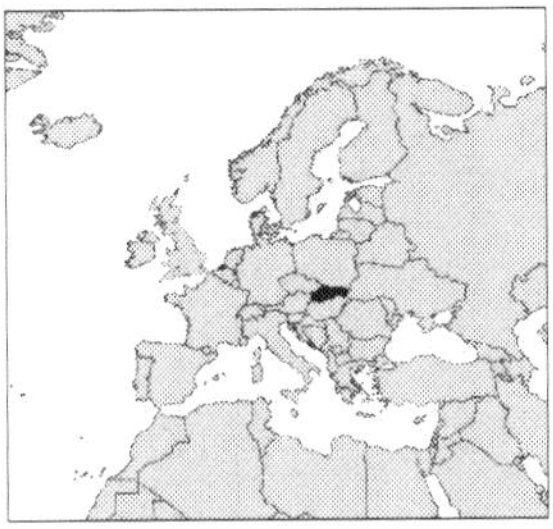

Slovakia in Europe

SLOVAKIA

Capital City: Bratislava
Area: 49,035km² (18,933 sq mi)
Population: 5,450,421
Highest Point: Gerlachovsky Stit (2655m)
Official Languages: Slovak
GDP: $117.40 billion
Currency: Euro
Major Religions: Christianity
Government: Unitary Parliamentary Republic
Geography: Temperate, Mountain
Time Zone: UTC+1
Major Cities: Bratislava, Kosice

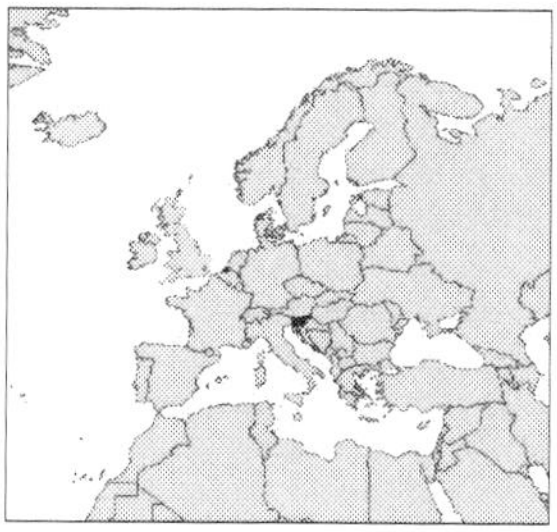

Slovenia in Europe

SLOVENIA

Capital City: Ljubljana
Area: 20,273km² (7827 sq mi)
Population: 2,080,906
Highest Point: Triglav (2864m)
Official Languages: Slovene
GDP: $54.00 billion
Currency: Euro
Major Religions: Christianity
Government: Unitary Parliamentary Constitutional Republic
Geography: Temperate
Time Zone: UTC+1
Major Cities: Ljubljana

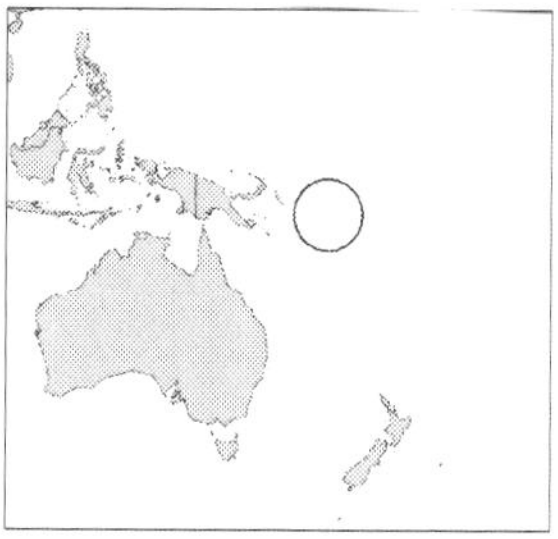

Solomon Islands in Australia & Oceania

SOLOMON ISLANDS

Capital City: Honiara
Area: 28,400 km² (11,000 sq mi)
Population: 599,419
Highest Point: Mt. Popomanaseu (2335m)
Official Languages: English
GDP: $1.51 billion
Currency: Solomon Islands Dollar
Major Religions: Christianity
Government: Unitary Parliamentary Constitutional Monarchy
Geography: Tropical
Time Zone: UTC+11
Major Cities: Honiara

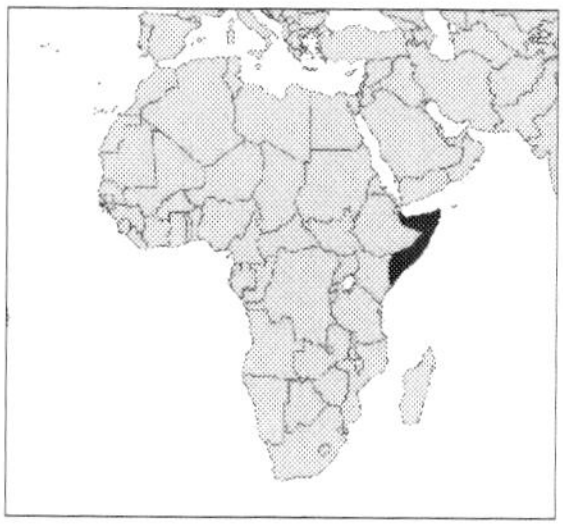

Somalia in Africa

SOMALIA

Capital City: Mogadishu
Area: 637,657km² (246,201 sq mi)
Population: 11,031,386
Highest Point: Shimbiris (2450m)
Official Languages: Somali/Arabic
GDP: $7.90 billion
Currency: Somali Shilling
Major Religions: Islam
Government: Federal Parliamentary Republic
Geography: Desert
Time Zone: UTC+3
Major Cities: Mogadishu, Hargeisa, Burco

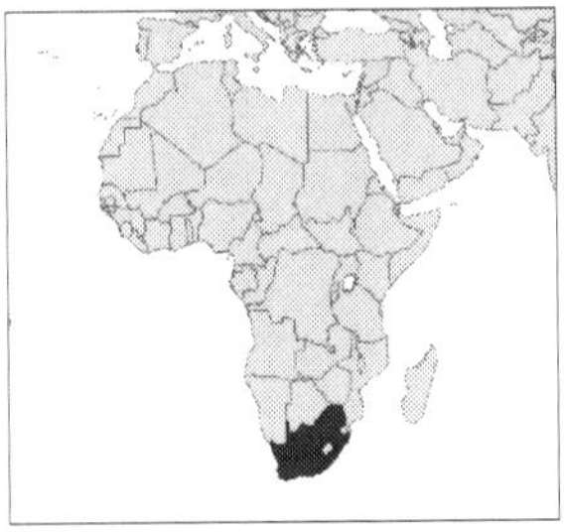

South Africa in Africa

SOUTH AFRICA

Capital City: Pretoria
Area: 1,221,037km² (471,445 sq mi)
Population: 57,725,600
Highest Point: Mafadi (3450m)
Official Languages: English +11 others
GDP: $371.30 billion
Currency: South African Rand
Major Religions: Christianity
Government: Unitary Parliamentary Constitutional Republic
Geography: Temperate, Meditteranean, Desert
Time Zone: UTC+2
Major Cities: Johannesburg, Cape Town, Durban, Pretoria, Port Elizabeth

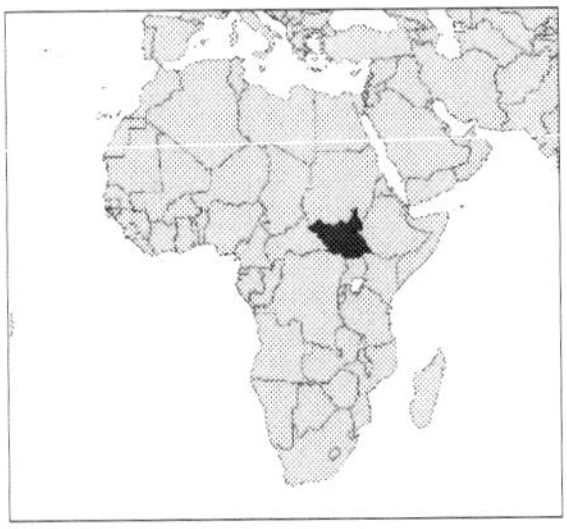

South Sudan in Europe

SOUTH SUDAN

Capital City: Juba
Area: 619,745 km² (239,285 sq mi)
Population: 12,230,730
Highest Point: Kinyeti (3187m)
Official Languages: English
GDP: $3.19 billion
Currency: South Sudanese Pound
Major Religions: Christianity
Government: Federal Presidential Constitutional Republic
Geography: Savanna, Tropical
Time Zone: UTC+3
Major Cities: Juba, Wau, Malakal, Yambia

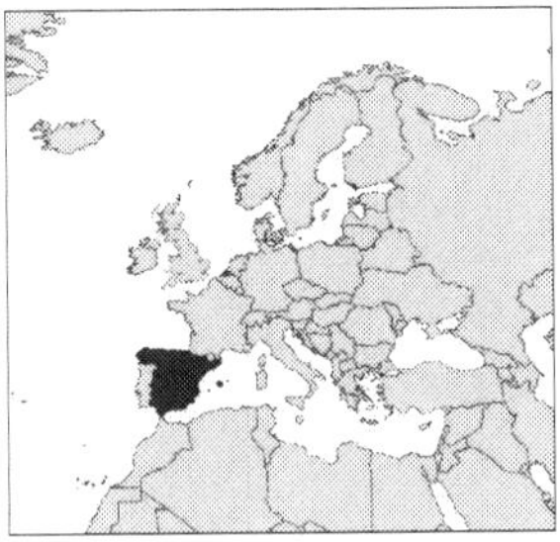

Spain in Europe

SPAIN

Capital City: Madrid
Area: 505,990 km² (195,360 sq mi)
Population: 46,934,632
Highest Point: Teide (3718m)
Official Languages: Spanish
GDP: $1398.00 billion
Currency: Euro
Major Religions: Christianity
Government: Unitary Parliamentary Costitutional Monarchy
Geography: Temperate, Mediterannean, Mountain
Time Zone: UTC+1
Major Cities: Madrid, Barcelona, Valencia, Seville, Zaragoza, Malaga

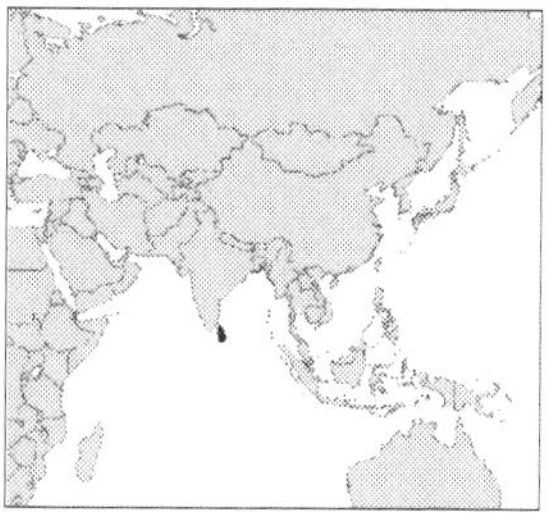

Sri Lanka in Asia

SRI LANKA

Capital City: Sri Jayawardenepura Kotte
Area: 65,610 km² (25,330 sq mi)
Population: 21,670,000
Highest Point: Pirdurutalagala (2524m)
Official Languages: Sinhala/Tamil
GDP: $371.30 billion
Currency: Sri Lankan Rupee
Major Religions: Buddhism
Government: Unitary Presidential Constitutional Republic
Geography: Tropical
Time Zone: UTC+5:30
Major Cities: Colombo, Kaduwela, Maharagama

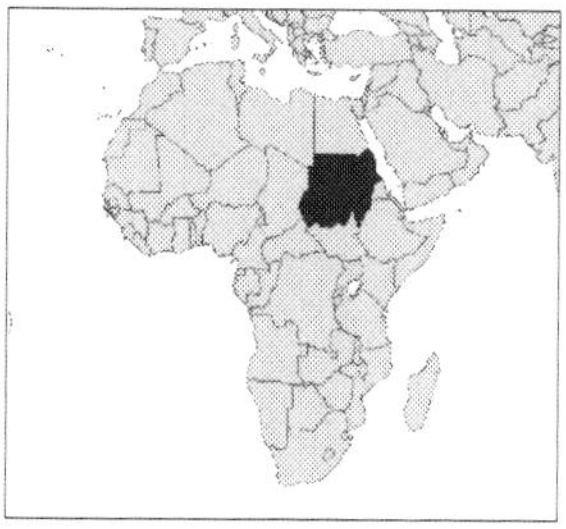

Sudan in Africa

SUDAN

Capital City: Khartoum
Area: 1,886,068 km² (728,215 sq mi)
Population: 41,592,539
Highest Point: Deriba Caldera (3042m)
Official Languages: Arabic/English
GDP: $33.90 billion
Currency: Sudanese Pound
Major Religions: Islam
Government: Federal Parliamentary Republic
Geography: Desert
Time Zone: UTC+2
Major Cities: Omdurman, Khartoum, Khartoum North

Suriname in South America

SURINAME

Capital City: Paramaribo
Area: 163,821 km² (63,252 sq mi)
Population: 558,368
Highest Point: Juliana Top (1230m)
Official Languages: Dutch
GDP: $4.11 billion
Currency: Surinamese Dollar
Major Religions: Christianity
Government: Unitary Republic
Geography: Tropical
Time Zone: UTC-3
Major Cities: Paramaribo

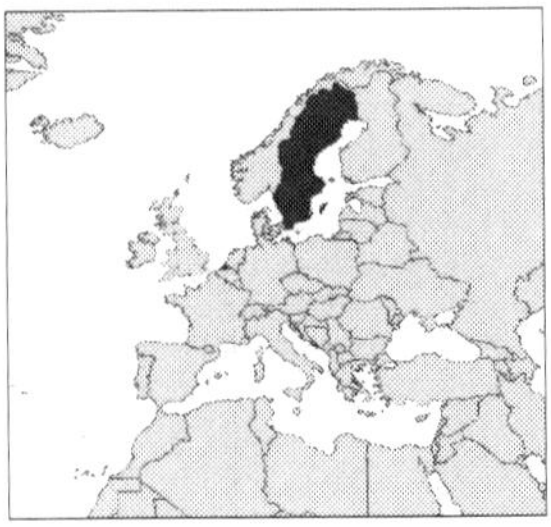

Sweden in Europe

SWEDEN

Capital City: Stockholm
Area: 450,295 km² (173,860 sq mi)
Population: 10,272,518
Highest Point: Kebnekaise (2097m)
Official Languages: Swedish
GDP: $563.00 billion
Currency: Swedish Krona
Major Religions: Christianity
Government: Unitary Presidential Constitutional Monarchy
Geography: Temperate, Taiga
Time Zone: UTC+1
Major Cities: Stockholm, Gothenburg, Malmo, Uppsala

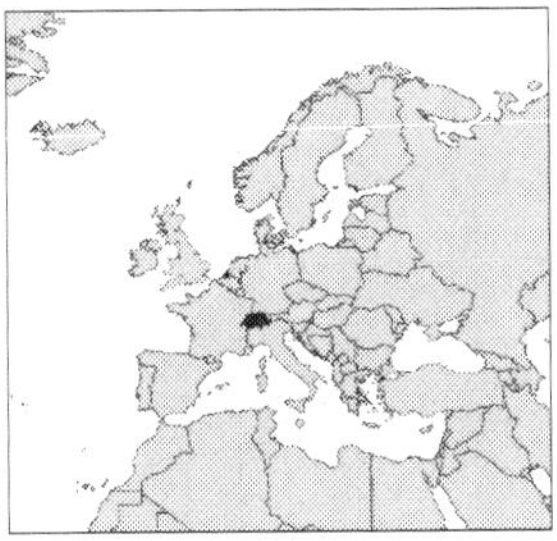

Switzerland in Europe

SWITZERLAND

Capital City: Bern
Area: 41,285 km² (15,940 sq mi)
Population: 8,508,898
Highest Point: Dufourspitze (4634m)
Official Languages: French/German/Italian /Romansh
GDP: $704.00 billion
Currency: Swiss Pound
Major Religions: Christianity
Government: Federal Democracy under a Parliamentary Directoral Republic
Geography: Temperate, Mountain
Time Zone: UTC+1
Major Cities: Zurich, Geneva, Basel, Lausanne, Bern

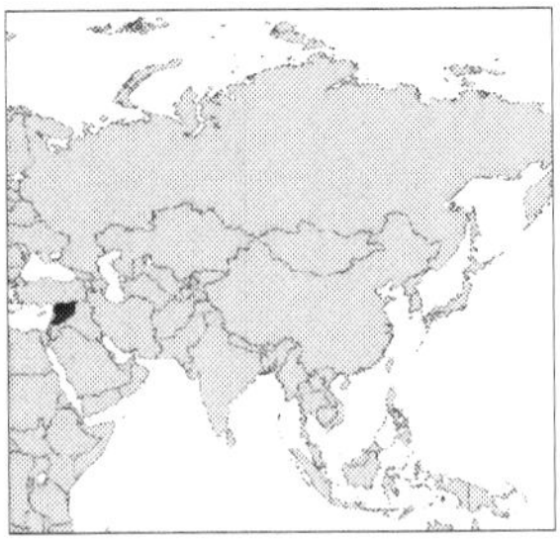

Syria in Asia

SYRIA

Capital City: Damascus
Area: 185,180 km² (71,500 sq mi)
Population: 18,503,159
Highest Point: Jabal El-Sheikh (2814m)
Official Languages: Arabic
GDP: $24.60 billion
Currency: Syrian Pound
Major Religions: Islam
Government: Unitary Presdiential Republic
Geography: Desert
Time Zone: UTC+2
Major Cities: Aleppo, Damascus, Homs, Latakia

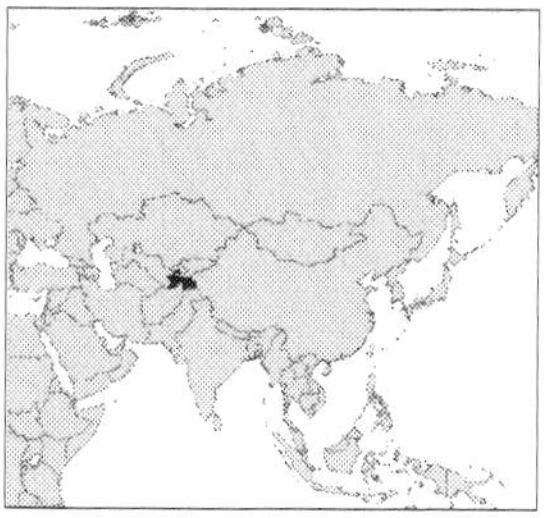

Tajikistan in Asia

TAJIKISTAN

Capital City: Dushanbe
Area: 143,100km² (55,300 sq mi)
Population: 9,275,827
Highest Point: Ismoil Somoni Peak (7495m)
Official Languages: Tajik
GDP: $7.35 billion
Currency: Somoni
Major Religions: Islam
Government: Unitary Presidential Constitutional Republic
Geography: Desert, Mountain
Time Zone: UTC+5
Major Cities: Dushanbe, Khujand

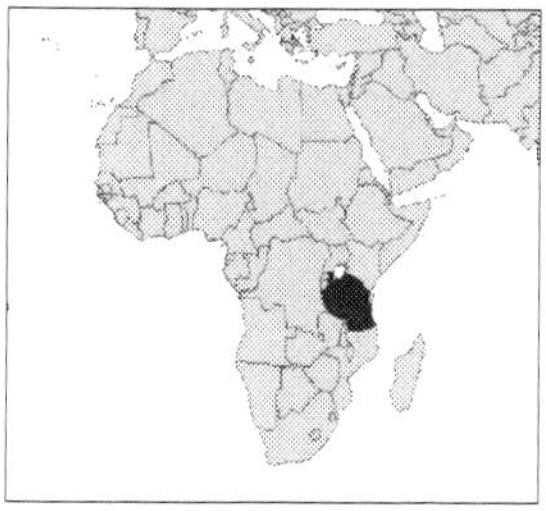

Tanzania in Africa

TANZANIA

Capital City: Dodoma
Area: 947,303 km² (365,756 sq mi)
Population: 55,572,201
Highest Point: Kilimanjaro (5892m)
Official Languages: English/Swahili
GDP: $61.03 billion
Currency: Tanzanian Shilling
Major Religions: Christianity
Government: Unitary Presidential Constitutional Republic
Geography: Tropical, Savanna, Mountain
Time Zone: UTC+3
Major Cities: Dar Es Salaam, Mwanza, Arusha, Dodoma

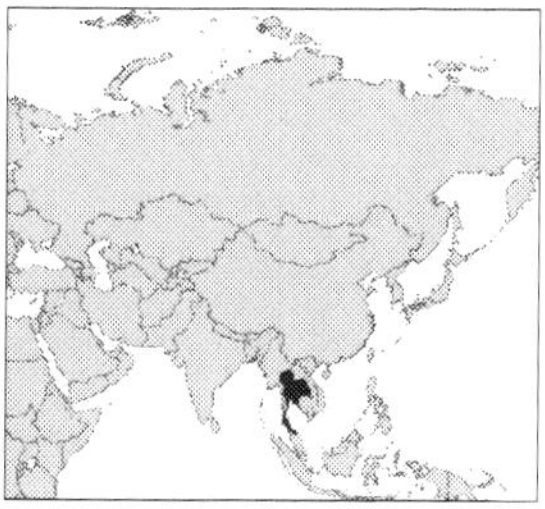

Thailand in Asia

THAILAND

Capital City: Bangkok
Area: 513,120 km² (198,120 sq mi)
Population: 68,863,514
Highest Point: Doi Inthanon (2565m)
Official Languages: Thai
GDP: $516.00 billion
Currency: Baht
Major Religions: Buddhism
Government: Unitary Parliamentary Constitutional Monarchy
Geography: Tropical
Time Zone: UTC+7
Major Cities: Bangkok, Nonthaburi City

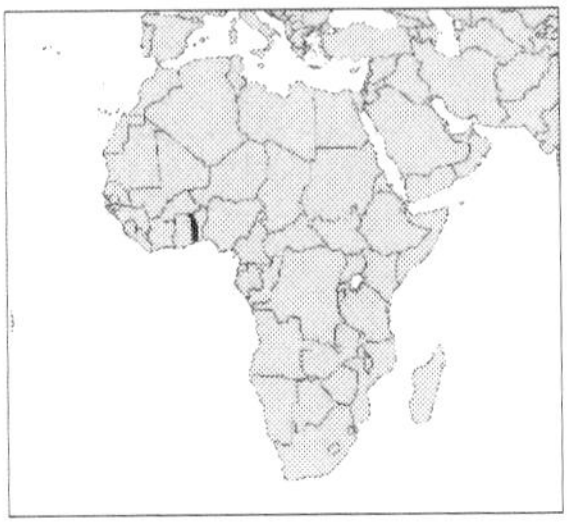

Togo in Africa

TOGO

Capital City: Lome
Area: 56,785 km² (21,925 sq mi)
Population: 7,965,055
Highest Point: Mont Agou (986m)
Official Languages: French
GDP: $5.59 billion
Currency: West African CFA Franc
Major Religions: Christianity
Government: Unitary Presidential Republic
Geography: Tropical, Savanna
Time Zone: UTC+0
Major Cities: Lome, Sokode

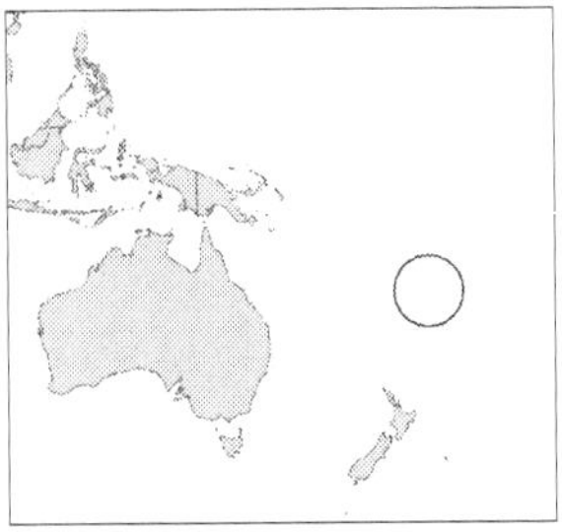

Tonga in Australia & Oceania

TONGA

Capital City: Nuku'alofa
Area: 748km² (289 sq mi)
Population: 100,651
Highest Point: Unnamed (1033m)
Official Languages: English/Tongan
GDP: $0.49 billion
Currency: Pa'anga
Major Religions: Christianity
Government: Unitary Parliamentary Constitutional Monarchy
Geography: Tropical
Time Zone: UTC+13
Major Cities: Nuku'alofa

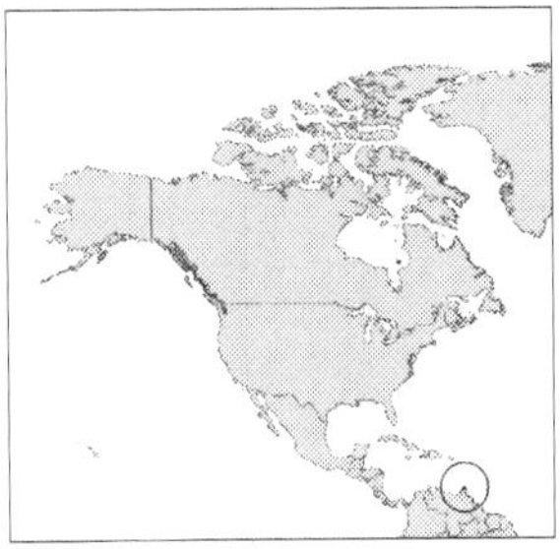

Trinidad and Tobago in North America

TRINIDAD AND TOBAGO

Capital City: Port Of Spain
Area: 5131 km² (1981 sq mi)
Population: 1,359,193
Highest Point: El Cerro del Aripo (940m)
Official Languages: English
GDP: $22.44 billion
Currency: Trinidad and Tobago Dollar
Major Religions: Christian
Government: Unitary Parliamentary Constitutional Republic
Geography: Tropical
Time Zone: UTC-4
Major Cities: Chaguanas, San Fernando, Port of Spain

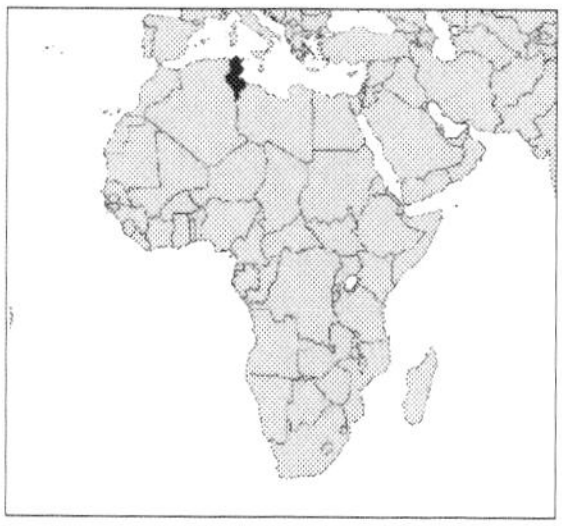

Tunisia in Africa

TUNISIA

Capital City: Tunis
Area: 163,610 km² (63,170 sq mi)
Population: 11,434,994
Highest Point: Jebel ech Chambi (1544m)
Official Languages: Arabic
GDP: $42.28 billion
Currency: Tunisian Dinar
Major Religions: Islam
Government: Unitary Presidential Republic
Geography: Desert, Mediterannean
Time Zone: UTC+0
Major Cities: Tunis, Sfax, Sousse

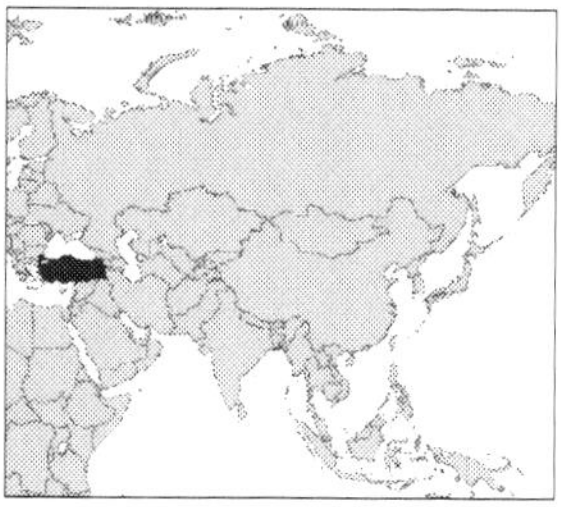

Turkey in Europe/Asia

TURKEY

Capital City: Ankara
Area: 783,356km² (302,455 sq mi)
Population: 82,003,882
Highest Point: Mt. Ararat (5137m)
Official Languages: Turkish
GDP: $743.71 billion
Currency: Turkish Lira
Major Religions: Islam
Government: Unitary Presidential Constitutional Republic
Geography: Mediterannean, Mountain, Temperate
Time Zone: UTC+3
Major Cities: Istanbul, Ankara, Izmir, Bursa, Adana, Gaziantep

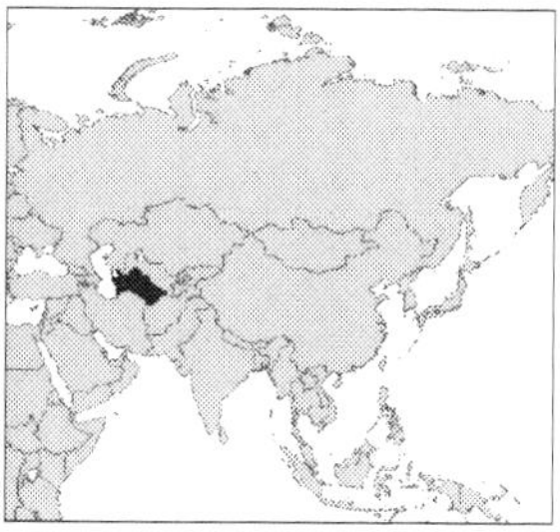

Turkmenistan in Asia

TURKMENISTAN

Capital City: Ashgabat
Area: 491,210km² (189,660 sq mi)
Population: 5,662,544
Highest Point: Ayrybaba (3139m)
Official Languages: Turkmen
GDP: $42.76 billion
Currency: Turkmen New Manat
Major Religions: Islam
Government: Unitary Parliamentary Republic under a dictatorship
Geography: Desert
Time Zone: UTC+5
Major Cities: Ashgabat, Turkmenabat, Dasoguz

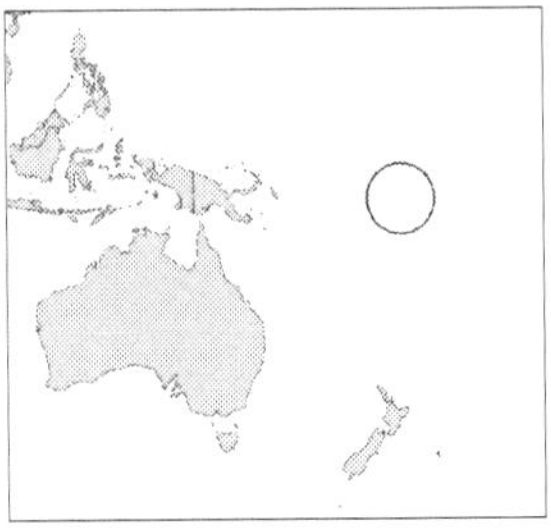

Tuvalu in Australia & Oceania

TUVALU

Capital City: Funafuti
Area: 26 km² (210 sq mi)
Population: 11,192
Highest Point: Unnamed (5m)
Official Languages: English/Tuvaluan
GDP: $0.03 billion
Currency: Tuvaluan Dollar, Australian Dollar
Major Religions: Christianity
Government: Unitary Parliamentary Constitutional Monarchy
Geography: Tropical
Time Zone: UTC+12
Major Cities: Funafuti

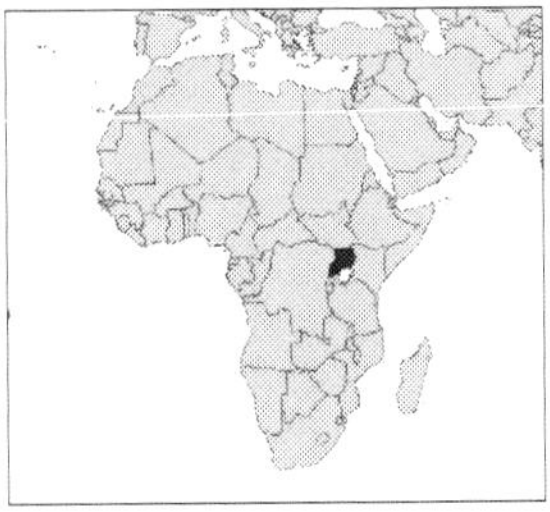

Uganda in Africa

UGANDA

Capital City: Kampala
Area: 241,038 km² (93,065 sq mi)
Population: 41,487,965
Highest Point: Mt. Stanley (5109m)
Official Languages: English/Swahili
GDP: $30.76 billion
Currency: Ugandan Shilling
Major Religions: Christianity
Government: Unitary Presidential Republic
Geography: Tropical, Mountain
Time Zone: UTC+3
Major Cities: Kampala, Nansana, Kira, Ssabagabo

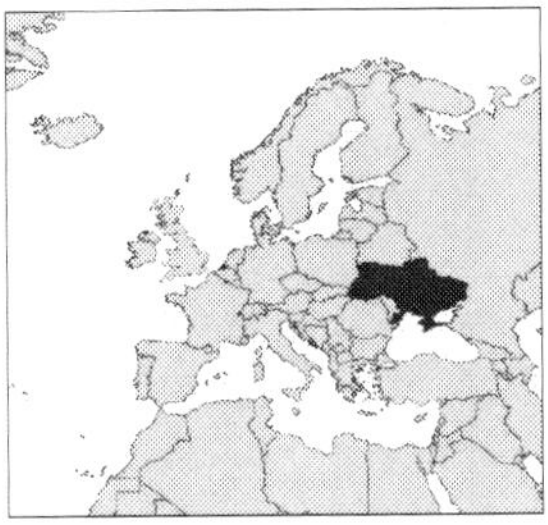

Ukraine in Europe

UKRAINE

Capital City: Kiev
Area: 603,628km² (233,062 sq mi)
Population: 42,418,235
Highest Point: Hoverla (2061m)
Official Languages: Ukrainian
GDP: $134.88 billion
Currency: Ukrainian Hryvnia
Major Religions: Irreligious
Government: Unitary Semi-Presidential Constitutional Republic
Geography: Temperate
Time Zone: UTC+2
Major Cities: Kiev, Kharkiv, Odessa, Dnipro, Donetsk

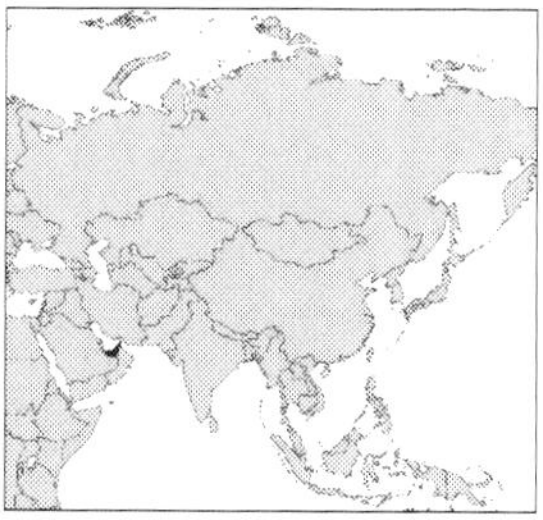

United Arab Emirates in Asia

UNITED ARAB EMIRATES

Capital City: Abu Dhabi
Area: 83,600km² (32,300 sq mi)
Population: 9,599,353
Highest Point: Jabal Al Jais (1910m)
Official Languages: Arabic
GDP: $432.61 billion
Currency: UAE Dirham
Major Religions: Islam
Government: Federal Elective Constitutional Monarchy
Geography: Desert
Time Zone: UTC+12
Major Cities: Dubai, Abu Dhabi, Sharjah

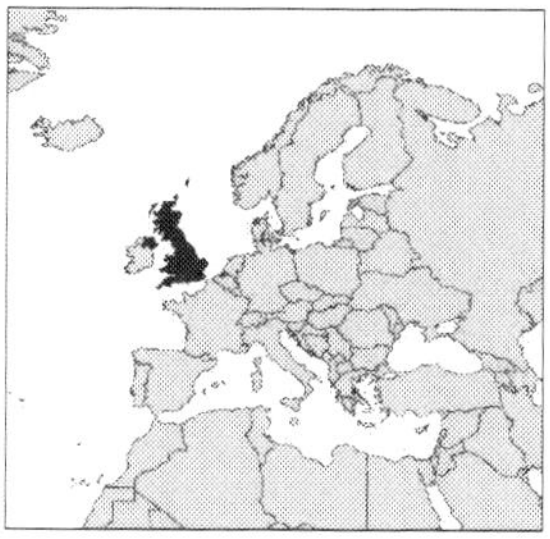

United Kingdom in Europe

UNITED KINGDOM

Capital City: London
Area: 242,495 km² (93,628 sq mi)
Population: 66,921,307
Highest Point: Ben Nevis (1345m)
Official Languages: English
GDP: $2744.00 billion
Currency: Pound Sterling
Major Religions: Christianity
Government: Unitary Parliamentary Constitutional Monarchy
Geography: Temperate
Time Zone: UTC+0
Major Cities: London, Birmingham, Manchester, Leeds, Glasgow

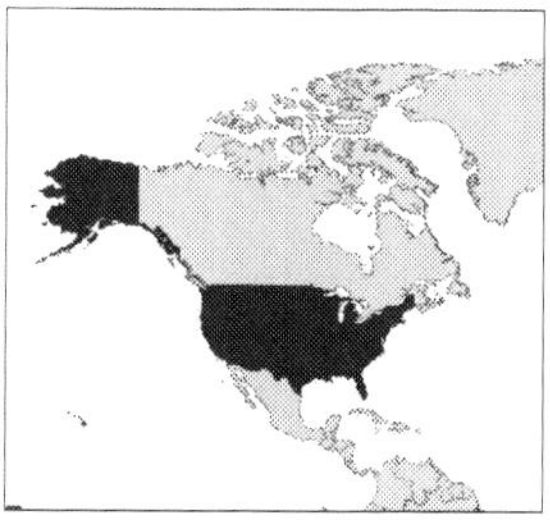

United States in North America / Oceania

UNITED STATES

Capital City: Washington D.C.
Area: 9,833,520km² (3,796,742 sq mi)
Population: 327,167,134
Highest Point: Denali (6191m)
Official Languages: (English)
GDP: $21439.00 billion
Currency: United States Dollar
Major Religions: Christianity
Government: Federal Presidential Constitutional Republic
Geography: Temperate, Desert, Mountain, Mediterannean, Taiga, Tundra
Time Zone: UTC-4 to -12,+10,+11
Major Cities: New York, Los Angeles, Chicago, Miami, Las Vegas, San Francisco, Seattle, Houston, Philadelphia, Phoenix, San Diego, Dallas

Uruguay in South America

URUGUAY

Capital City: Montevideo
Area: 176,215km² (68,037 sq mi)
Population: 3,444,006
Highest Point: Cerro Catedral (514m)
Official Languages: Spanish
GDP: $59.92 billion
Currency: Uruguayan Peso
Major Religions: Christianity, Irreligious
Government: Unitary Presidential Constitutional Republic
Geography: Temperate
Time Zone: UTC-3
Major Cities: Montevideo

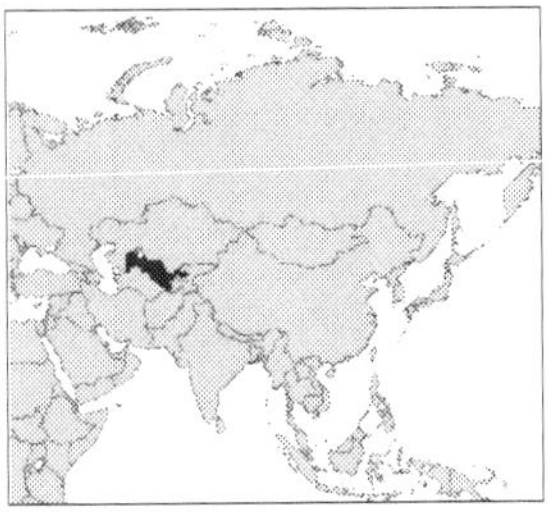

Uzbekistan in Asia

UZBEKISTAN

Capital City: Tashkent
Area: 448,798 km² (173,351 sq mi)
Population: 32,768,725
Highest Point: Khazret Sultan (4643m)
Official Languages: Uzbek
GDP: $49.12 billion
Currency: Uzbek Som
Major Religions: Islam
Government: Unitary Presdiential Constitutional Republic
Geography: Desert, Mountain
Time Zone: UTC+5
Major Cities: Tashkent, Samarqand, Namangan

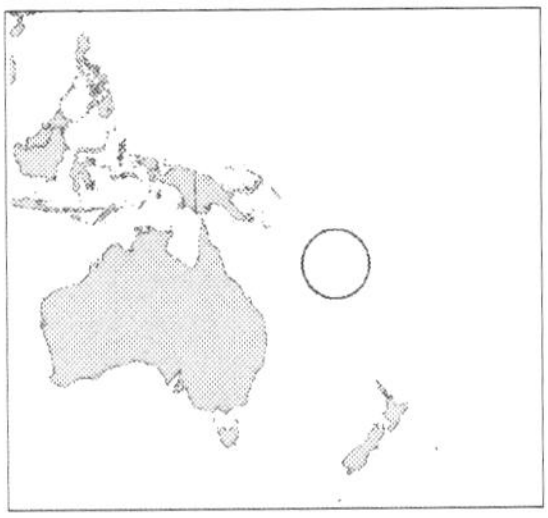

Vanuatu in Australia & Oceania

VANUATU

Capital City: Port Vila
Area: 12,189 km² (4,706 sq mi)
Population: 272,459
Highest Point: Mt. Tabwemasana (1877m)
Official Languages: Bislama/English/ French
GDP: $0.96 billion
Currency: Vanuatu Vatu
Major Religions: Christianity
Government: Unitary Parliamentary Republic
Geography: Tropical
Time Zone: UTC+11
Major Cities: Port Vila

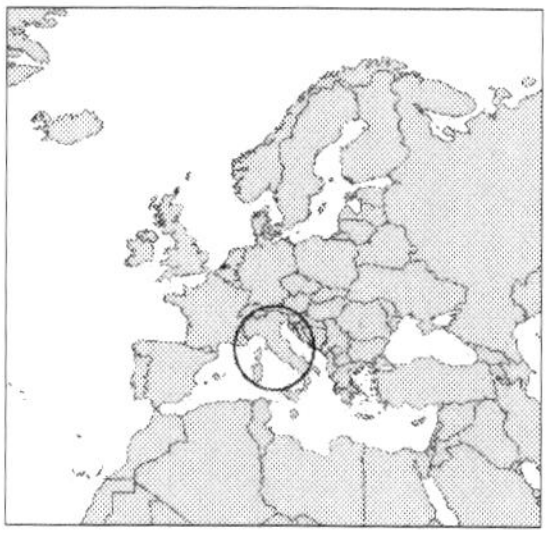

Vatican City in Europe

VATICAN CITY

Capital City: Vatican City
Area: 0.4km² (0.2 sq mi)
Population: 1000
Highest Point: Vatican Hill (75m)
Official Languages: Italian/Latin
GDP: -
Currency: Euro
Major Religions: Christianity
Government: Unitary Absolute Monarchy under an Ecclesiastical, Elective Theocracy
Geography: Mediterranean
Time Zone: UTC+1
Major Cities: Vatican City

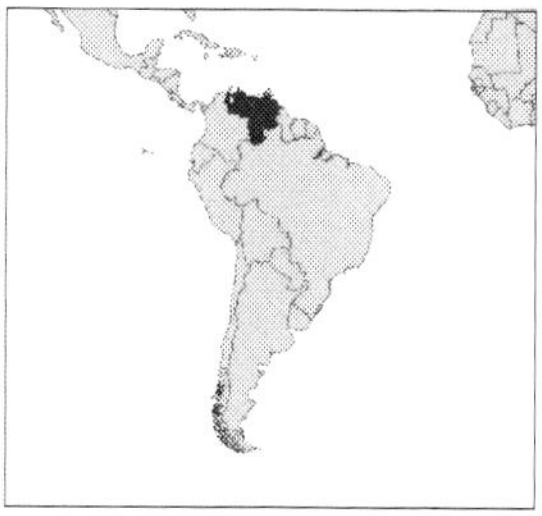

Venezuela in South America

VENEZUELA

Capital City: Caracas
Area: 916,445km² (353,841 sq mi)
Population: 31,568,179
Highest Point: Pico Bolivar (4978m)
Official Languages: Spanish
GDP: $70.14 billion
Currency: Bolivar Soberano
Major Religions: Christianity
Government: Federal Presdiential Constitutional Republic
Geography: Tropical, Mountain
Time Zone: UTC-4
Major Cities: Caracas, Maracaibo, Valencia, Barquisimeto

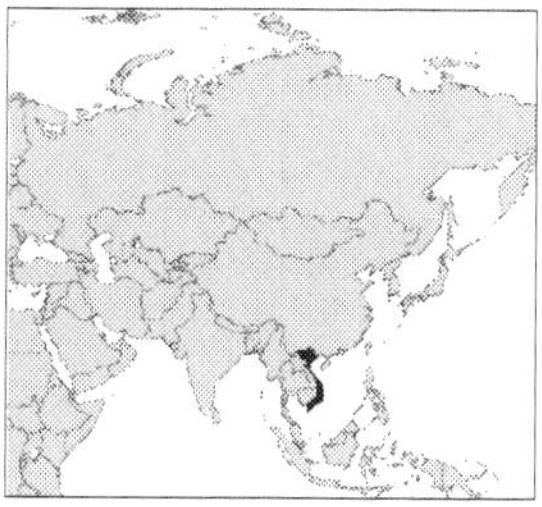

Vietnam in Asia

VIETNAM

Capital City: Hanoi
Area: 331,212 km² (127,882 sq mi)
Population: 94,569,072
Highest Point: Fan Si Pan (3143m)
Official Languages: (Vietnamese)
GDP: $261.64 billion
Currency: Dong
Major Religions: Vietnamese Folk, Irreligious
Government: Unitary Marxist-Leninist One Party Socialist Republic
Geography: Tropical
Time Zone: UTC+7
Major Cities: Ho Chi Minh City, Hanoi, Hai Phong, Da Nang, Can Tho, Bien Hoa

YEMEN

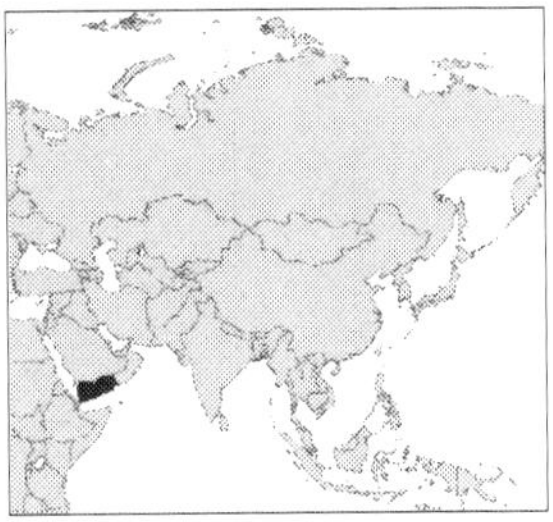

Yemen in Asia

Capital City: Sana'a
Area: 527,968 km² (203,850 sq mi)
Population: 27,584,213
Highest Point: Jabal An-Nabi Shu'ayb (3666m)
Official Languages: Arabic
GDP: $28.52 billion
Currency: Yemeni Rial
Major Religions: Islam
Government: Unitary Presidential Constitutional Republic
Geography: Mountain, Desert
Time Zone: UTC+3
Major Cities: Sana'a, Aden, Taiz, Al Hudaydah

ZAMBIA

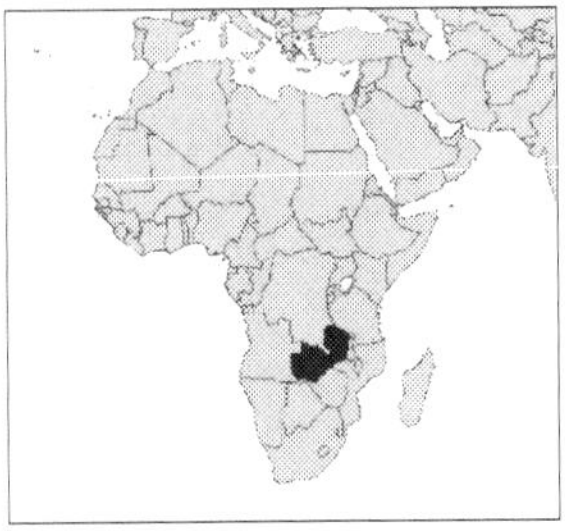

Zambia in Africa

Capital City: Lusaka
Area: 752,618 km² (290,587 sq mi)
Population: 16,591,390
Highest Point: Magfina Central (2329m)
Official Languages: English
GDP: $23.14 billion
Currency: Zambian Kwacha
Major Religions: Christianity
Government: Unitary Presdiential Constitutional Republic
Geography: Tropical
Time Zone: UTC+2
Major Cities: Lusaka, Kitwe, Ndola

ZIMBABWE

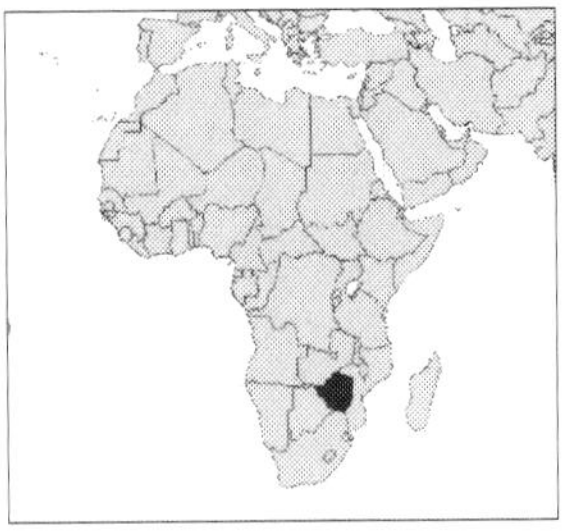

Zimbabwe in Africa

Capital City: Harare
Area: 390,757km² (150,872 sq mi)
Population: 16,150,362
Highest Point: Mt. Nyangani (2592m)
Official Languages: English (+16 others)
GDP: $22.29 billion
Currency: Zimbabwean Dollar
Major Religions: Christianity
Government: Unitary Presidential Constitutional Republic
Geography: Tropical, Savanna
Time Zone: UTC+3
Major Cities: Harare, Bulawayo, Chitungwiza

Countries Arranged By...

SIZE

1. **RUSSIA** – 17,098,246km^2 (6,601,670 sq mi)
2. **CANADA** – 9,984,670km^2 (3,855,100 sq mi)
3. **UNITED STATES** – 9,833,520km^2 (3,796,742 sq mi)
4. **CHINA** – 9,596,961km^2 (3,705,407 sq mi)
5. **BRAZIL** – 8,515,767km^2 (3,287,956 sq mi)
6. **AUSTRALIA** – 7,692,024km^2 (2,969,907 sq mi)
7. **INDIA** – 3,287,263km^2 (1,269,219 sq mi)
8. **ARGENTINA** – 2,780,400km^2 (1,073,500 sq mi)
9. **KAZAKHSTAN** – 2,724,900km^2 (1,052,100 sq mi)
10. **ALGERIA** – 2,381,741km^2 (919,945 sq mi)
11. **CONGO, DEMOCRATIC REPUBLIC OF** – 2,345,409km^2 (905,567 sq mi)
12. **SAUDI ARABIA** – 2,149,690km^2 (830,000 sq mi)
13. **MEXICO** – 1,964,375km^2 (758,449 sq mi)
14. **INDONESIA** – 1,910,931km^2 (737,815sq mi)
15. **SUDAN** – 1,861,484km^2 (718,723 sq mi)
16. **LIBYA** – 1,759,540km^2 (679,360 sq mi)
17. **IRAN** – 1,648,195km^2 (636,372 sq mi)
18. **MONGOLIA** – 1,564,110km^2 (603,910 sq mi)
19. **PERU** – 1,285,216km^2 (496,225 sq mi)
20. **CHAD** –1,284,000km^2 (496,000 sq mi)

POPULATION

1. **CHINA** – 1,430,000,000
2. **INDIA** – 1,370,000,000
3. **UNITED STATES** – 329,000,000
4. **INDONESIA** – 271,000,000
5. **PAKISTAN** – 217,000,000
6. **BRAZIL** – 211,000,000
7. **NIGERIA** – 201,000,000
8. **BANGLADESH** – 163,000,000

9. RUSSIA – 146,000,000
10. MEXICO – 128,000,000
11. JAPAN – 127,000,000
12. ETHIOPIA -112,000,000
13. PHILIPPINES – 108,000,000
14. EGYPT – 100,000,000
15. VIETNAM – 97,000,000
16. CONGO, DEMOCRATIC REPUBLIC OF – 87,000,000
17. GERMANY – 84,000,000
18. TURKEY – 83,000,000
19. IRAN – 83,000,000
20. THAILAND – 69,000,000

GDP

1. UNITED STATES – $21,439bn
2. CHINA – $14,140bn
3. JAPAN – $5154bn
4. GERMANY – $3863bn
5. INDIA – $2936bn
6. UNITED KINGDOM – $2744bn
7. FRANCE – $2707bn
8. ITALY – $1989bn
9. BRAZIL – $1847bn
10. CANADA – $1731bn
11. RUSSIA – $1638bn
12. KOREA, SOUTH – $1630bn
13. SPAIN – $1398bn
14. AUSTRALIA – $1376bn
15. MEXICO – $1274bn
16. INDONESIA – $1111bn
17. NETHERLANDS – $902bn
18. SAUDI ARABIA – $779bn

19. **TURKEY** – $744bn
20. **SWITZERLAND** – $715bn

HIGHEST POINT

1. **CHINA/NEPAL** – Mount Everest (8848m)
2. **PAKISTAN** – K2 (8611m)
3. **INDIA** – Kangchenjunga (8586m)
4. **BHUTAN** – Gangkhar Puensum (7570m)
5. **TAJIKISTAN** – Ismoil Somoni Peak (7495m)
6. **AFGHANISTAN** – Noshaq (7492m)
7. **KYRGYZSTAN** – Jengish Chokusu (7439m)
8. **KAZAKHSTAN** – Khan Tengri (7010m)
9. **ARGENTINA** – Aconcagua (6962m)
10. **CHILE** – Ojos Del Salado (6893m)
11. **PERU** – Huascaran (6768m)
12. **BOLIVIA** – Sajama (6542m)
13. **ECUADOR** – Chimborazo (6267m)
14. **UNITED STATES** – Denali (6190m)
15. **CANADA** – Mount Logan (5959m)
16. **TANZANIA** – Kilimanjaro (5892m)
17. **MYANMAR** – Hkakabo Razi (5881m)
18. **COLOMBIA** – Pico Cristobal Colon (5700m)
19. **RUSSIA** – Mount Elbrus (5642m)
20. **MEXICO** – Pico De Orizaba (5636m)

World Geography

World's Oceans and Seas

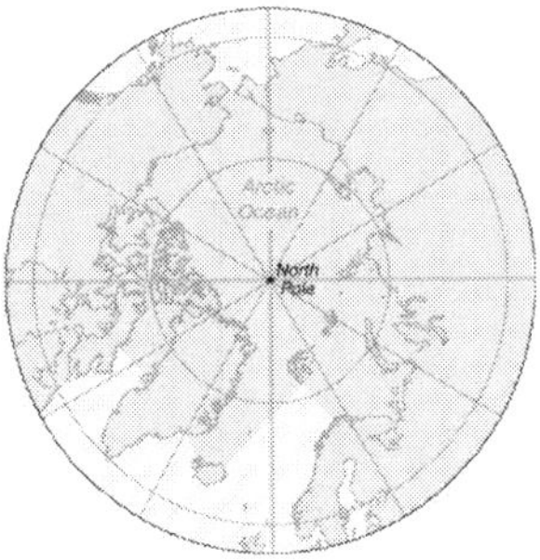

ARCTIC OCEAN

- CHUKCHI SEA
- EAST SIBERIAN SEA
- LAPTEV SEA
- KARA SEA
- BARENTS SEA
- QUEEN VCTORIA SEA
- WANDEL SEA
- GREENLAND SEA
- BAFFIN BAY
- HUDSON BAY
- BEAUFORT SEA

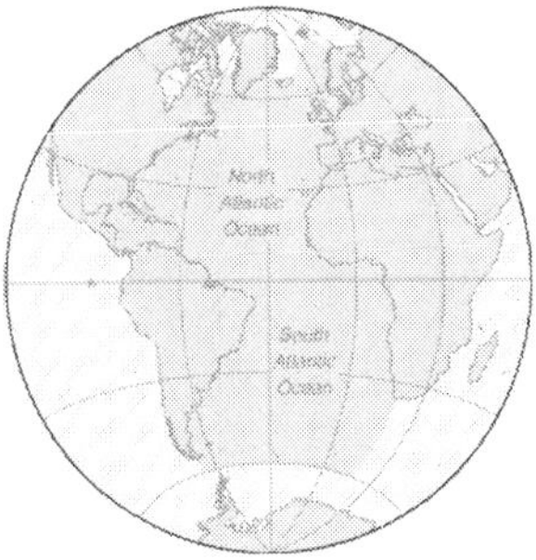

ATLANTIC OCEAN

- LABRADOR SEA
- GULF OF MEXICO
- CARIBBEAN SEA
- ARGENTINE SEA
- NORWEIGAN SEA
- NORTH SEA
- BALTIC SEA
- IRISH SEA
- CELTIC SEA
- BAY OF BISCAY
- MEDITERRANEAN SEA
  - ADRIATIC SEA
  - AEGEAN SEA
  - ALBORAN SEA
  - BALEARIC SEA
  - IONIAN SEA
  - LEVANTINE SEA
  - LIBYAN SEA
  - LIGUARIAN SEA
  - TYRRHENIAN SEA
- BLACK SEA
- SEA OF AZOV

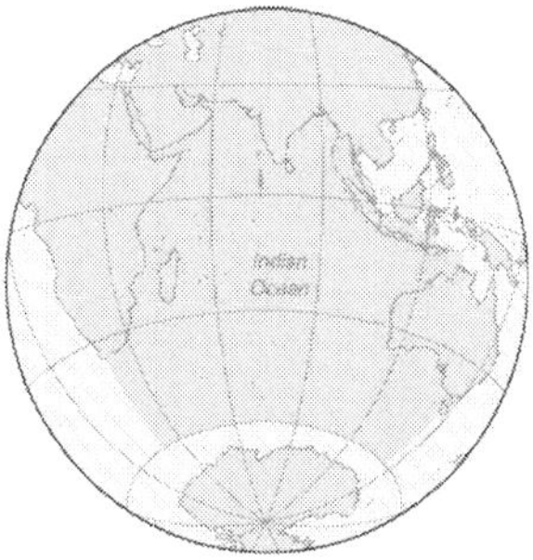

INDIAN OCEAN

- ANDAMAN SEA
- ARABIAN SEA
- BAY OF BENGAL
- LACCADIVE SEA
- PERSIAN GULF
- RED SEA
- TIMOR SEA

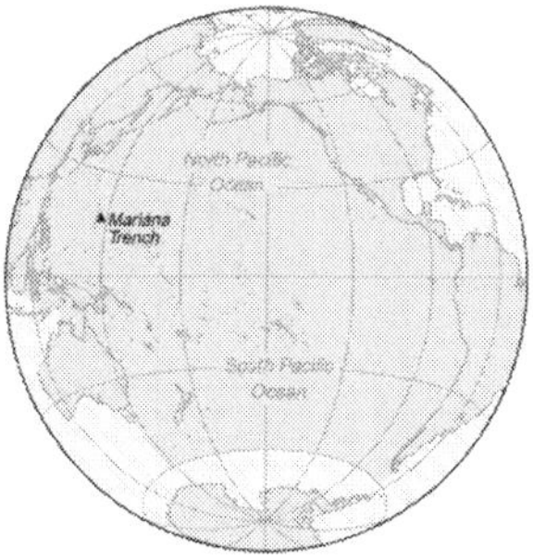

PACIFIC OCEAN

- BERING SEA
- CHILEAN SEA
- GULF OF CALIFORNIA
- GRAU SEA
- SALISH SEA
- ARAFURA SEA
- BALI SEA
- BANDA SEA
- BISMARCK SEA
- BOHAI SEA
- BOHOL SEA
- CAMOTES SEA
- CELEBES SEA
- CERAM SEA
- CORAL SEA
- EAST CHINA SEA
- FLORES SEA
- GULF OF CARPENTARIA
- GULF OF THAILAND
- HALMAHERA SEA
- JAVA SEA
- KORO SEA
- MOLUCCA SEA
- PHILIPPINE SEA
- SAVU SEA
- SEA OF JAPAN
- SEA OF OKHOTSK
- SOLOMON SEA
- SOUTH CHINA SEA
- SULU SEA
- TASMAN SEA
- VISAYAN SEA
- YELLOW SEA

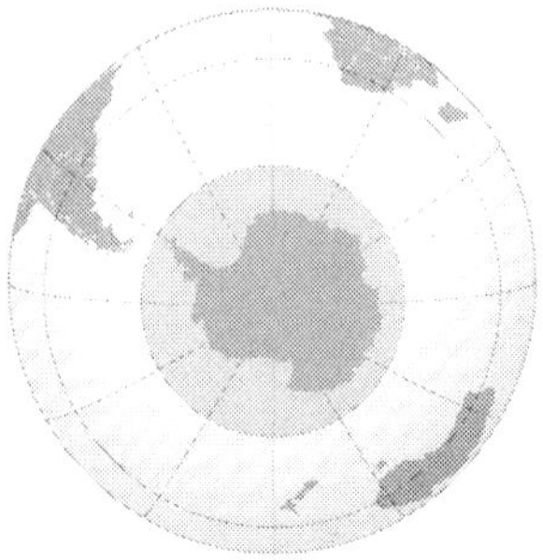

SOUTHERN OCEAN

- AMUNDSEN SEA
- BELLINGSHAUSEN SEA
- COOPERATION SEA
- COSMONAUTS SEA
- DAVIS SEA
- D'URVILLE SEA
- DRAKE PASSAGE
- KING HAAKON VII SEA
- LAZAREV SEA
- MAWSON SEA
- RIISER-LARSEN SEA
- ROSS SEA
- SCOTIA SEA
- SOMOV SEA
- WEDDELL SEA

World's Largest Deserts

	DESERT	CONTINENT	SIZE in KM^2 (Sq Mi)
1.	ANTARCTICA	*ANTARCTICA*	14,000,000 (5,500,000)
2.	ARCTIC	*EUROPE, ASIA, NORTH AMERICA*	13,985,000 (5,400,000)
3.	SAHARA DESERT	*AFRICA*	9,000,000 (3,300,000)
4.	AUSTRALIAN DESERT	*AUSTRALIA & OCEANIA*	2,700,000 (1,000,000)
5.	ARABIAN DESERT	*ASIA*	2,330,000 (900,000)
6.	GOBI DESERT	*ASIA*	1,295,000 (500,000)
7.	CALAHARI DESERT	*AFRICA*	900,000 (360,000)
8.	PATAGONIAN DESERT	*SOUTH AMERICA*	620,000 (265,000)
9.	SYRIAN DESERT	*ASIA*	520,000 (200,000)
10.	GREAT BASIN	*NORTH AMERICA*	492,000 (190,000)
11.	CHIHUAHUAN DESERT	*NORTH AMERICA*	450,000 (175,000)
12.	KARAKUM DESERT	*ASIA*	350,000 (135,000)
13.	COLORADO PLATEAU	*NORTH AMERICA*	337,000 (130,000)
14.	SONORAN DESERT	*NORTH AMERICA*	310,000 (120,000)
15.	KYZYLKUM DESERT	*ASIA*	300,000 (115,000)
16.	TAKLAMAKAN DESERT	*ASIA*	270,000 (105,000)

	DESERT	CONTINENT	SIZE in KM^2 (SQ MI)
17.	THAR DESERT	*ASIA*	200,000 (77,000)
18.	DASHT-E MARGO	*ASIA*	150,000 (58,000)
19.	REGISTAN DESERT	*ASIA*	146,000 (56,400)
20.	ATACAMA DESERT	*SOUTH AMERICA*	140,000 (54,000)
21.	MOJAVE DESERT	*NORTH AMERICA*	124,000 (48,000)
22.	COLUMBIA BASIN	*NORTH AMERICA*	83,100 (32,100)
23.	NAMIB DESERT	*AFRICA*	81,000 (31,000)
24.	DASHT-E KAVIR	*ASIA*	77,000 (30,000)
25.	DASHT-E LOOT	*ASIA*	52,000 (20,100)

World's Largest Islands

	ISLAND	COUNTRY	SIZE in KM² (SQ MI)
1.	GREENLAND	*DENMARK*	2,130,800 (822,700)
2.	NEW GUINEA	*INDONESIA/PAPUA NEW GUINEA*	785,753 (28,251)
3.	BORNEO	*INDONESIA/ MALAYSIA/BRUNEI*	748,168 (288,869)
4.	MADAGASCAR	*MAADAGASCAR*	587,041 (226,658)
5.	BAFFIN ISLAND	*CANADA*	507,451 (195,928)
6.	SUMATRA	*INDONESIA*	443,065 (171,068)
7.	HONSHU	*JAPAN*	225,800 (87,200)
8.	VICTORIA ISLAND	*CANADA*	217,291 (83,897)
9.	GREAT BRITAIN	*UNITED KINGDOM*	209,331 (80,823)
10.	ELLESMERE ISLAND	*CANADA*	196,236 (75,767)
11.	SULAWESI	*INDONESIA*	180,681 (69,761)
12.	SOUTH ISLAND	*NEW ZEALAND*	145,836 (56,308)
13.	JAVA	*INDONESIA*	138,794 (53,589)
14.	NORTH ISLAND	*NEW ZEALAND*	111,583 (43,082)
15.	LUZON	*PHILLIPINES*	109,965 (42,458)
16.	NEWFOUNDLAND	*CANADA*	108,860 (42,030)

	ISLAND	COUNTRY	SIZE in KM^2 (SQ MI)
17.	CUBA	*CUBA*	105,806 (40,582)
18.	ICELAND	*ICELAND*	101,826 (39,315)
19.	MINDANAO	*PHILLIPINES*	97,530 (37,660)
20.	IRELAND	*IRELAND/UNITED KINGDOM*	84,421 (32,595)
21.	HOKKAIDO	*JAPAN*	78,719 (30,394)
22.	HISPANIOLA	*HAITI/DOMINICAN REPUBLIC*	73,929 (28,544)
23.	SAKHALIN	*RUSSIA*	72,493 (27,990)
24.	BANKS ISLAND	*CANADA*	70,028 (27,038)
25.	SRI LANKA	*SRI LANKA*	65,268 (25,200)
26.	TASMANIA	*AUSTRALIA*	65,022 (25,105)
27.	DEVON ISLAND	*CANADA*	55,247 (21,331)
28.	ALEXANDER ISLAND	*NONE (ANTARCTICA)*	49,070 (18,950)
29.	ISLA GRANDE DE TIERRA DEL FUEGO	*ARGENTINA/ CHILE*	47,992 (18,530)
30.	SEVERNY ISLAND	*RUSSIA*	47,079 (18,177)
31.	BERKNER ISLAND	*NONE (ANTARCTICA)*	43,873 (16,939)
32.	AXEL HEIBERG ISLAND	*CANADA*	43,178 (16,671)
33.	MELVILLE ISLAND	*CANADA*	42,149 (16,274)

	ISLAND	COUNTRY	SIZE in KM² (SQ MI)
34.	SOUTHAMPTON ISLAND	*CANADA*	41,214 (15,913)
35.	MARAJO	*BRAZIL*	40,100 (15,500)
36.	SPITSBERGEN	*NORWAY*	38,981 (15,051)
37.	KYUSHU	*JAPAN*	37,437 (14,455)
38.	NEW BRITAIN	*PAPUA NEW GUINEA*	35,145 (13,570)
39.	TAIWAN	*TAIWAN*	34,507 (13,323)
40.	PRINCE OF WALES ISLAND	*CANADA*	33,339 (12,872)
41.	YUZHNY ISLAND	*RUSSIA*	33,246 (12,836)
42.	HAINAN	*CHINA*	33,210 (12,820)
43.	VANCOUVER ISLAND	*INDIA*	31,285 (12,079)
44.	TIMOR	*INDONESIA*	28,418 (10,972)
45.	SICILY	*ITALY*	25,711 (9927)
46.	SOMERSET ISLAND	*CANADA*	24,786 (9570)
47.	KOTELNY ISLAND	*RUSSIA*	24,000 (9300)
48.	SARDINIA	*ITALY*	23,949 (9247)
49.	BANANAL	*BRAZIL*	20,000 (7398)
50.	SHIKOKU	*JAPAN*	18,545 (7160)

Other Principal Islands

	ISLAND	COUNTRY	SIZE in KM^2 (SQ MI)
53.	NEW CALEDONIA	*FRANCE*	16,648 (6428)
54.	BATHURST ISLAND	*CANADA*	16,042 (6194)
60.	FLORES	*INDONESIA*	14,154 (5465)
62.	NEGROS	*PHILIPPINES*	13,075 (5048)
70.	JAMAICA	*JAMAICA*	11,190 (4320)
74.	VITI LEVU	*FIJI*	10,531 (4066)
75.	HAWAI'I	*UNITED STATES*	10,434 (4029)
80.	CYPRUS	*CYPRUS/TURKEYU NITED KINGDOM*	9234 (3565)
81.	PUERTO RICO	*UNITED STATES*	9100 (3500)
83.	CORSICA	*FRANCE*	8741 (3375)
88.	CRETE	*GREECE*	8350 (3220)
95.	EAST FALKLAND	*UNITED KINGDOM*	7040 (2720)
96.	ZEALAND	*DENMARK*	7031 (2715)
108.	BALI	*INDONESIA*	5416 (2091)
117.	TRINIDAD	*TRINIDAD & TOBAGO*	5009 (1934)
124.	WEST FALKLAND	*UNITED KINGDOM*	4531 (1749)

	ISLAND	COUNTRY	SIZE in KM^2 (SQ MI)
131.	KANGAROO ISLAND	*AUSTRALIA*	4374 (1689)
147.	MALLORCA	*SPAIN*	3667 (1416)
149.	LONG ISLAND	*UNITED STATES*	3629 (1401)
150.	SOCOTRA	*YEMEN*	3607 (1393)
164.	GOTLAND	*SWEDEN*	2994 (1156)
201.	LEWIS AND HARRIS	*UNITED KINGDOM*	2086 (805)
208.	TENERIFE	*SPAIN*	2008 (775)
217.	MAURITIUS	*MAURITIUS*	1874 (724)
246.	OAHU	*UNITED STATES*	1583 (9300)
247.	ZANZIBAR (UNGUJA)	*TANZANIA*	1575 (608)
266.	RHODES	*GREECE*	1410 (540)
306.	GRAND BAHAMA	*BAHAMAS*	1096 (423)
309.	TAHITI	*FRANCE*	1069 (413)
-	IBIZA	*SPAIN*	572 (220)
-	MYKONOS	*GREECE*	250 (96)
-	MALTA	*MALTA*	246 (95)
-	EASTER ISLAND	*CHILE*	164 (63)

World's Largest Lakes

	LAKE	CONTINENT	SIZE in KM^2 (SQ MI)
1.	CASPIAN SEA	*ASIA*	371,000 (143,000)
2.	LAKE SUPERIOR	*NORTH AMERICA*	82,100 (31,700)
3.	LAKE VICTORIA	*AFRICA*	68,700 (26,590)
4.	LAKE HURON	*NORTH AMERICA*	59,600 (23,000)
5.	LAKE MICHIGAN	*NORTH AMERICA*	58,000 (22,000)
6.	TANGANYIKA	*AFRICA*	32,600 (12,600)
7.	BAIKAL	*ASIA*	31,500 (12,200)
8.	GREAT BEAR LAKE	*NORTH AMERICA*	31,000 (12,000)
9.	MALAWI	*AFRICA*	29,500 (11,400)
10.	GREAT SLAVE LAKE	*NORTH AMERICA*	27,000 (10,000)
11.	ERIE	*NORTH AMERICA*	25,700 (9900)
12.	WINNIPEG	*NORTH AMERICA*	24,514 (9465)
13.	ONTARIO	*NORTH AMERICA*	18,960 (7320)
14.	LADOGA	*EUROPE*	18,130 (7000)
15.	BALKHASH	*ASIA*	16,400 (6300)
16.	VOSTOK	*ANTARCTICA*	12,500 (4800)

	LAKE	CONTINENT	SIZE in KM² (SQ MI)
17.	ONEGA	*EUROPE*	9700 (3700)
18.	TITICACA	*SOUTH AMERICA*	8372 (3232)
19.	NICARAGUA	*NORTH AMERICA*	8264 (3191)
20.	ATHABASCA	*NORTH AMERICA*	7850 (3030)
21.	TAYMYR	*ASIA*	6990 (2700)
22.	TURKANA	*AFRICA*	6405 (2473)
23.	REINDEER LAKE	*NORTH AMERICA*	6330 (2440)
24.	ISSYK-KUL	*ASIA*	6200 (2400)
25.	URMIA	*ASIA*	6001 (2317)
26.	VANERN	*EUROPE*	5545 (2141)
27.	WINNIPEGOSIS	*NORTH AMERICA*	5403 (2086)
28.	ALBERT	*AFRICA*	5299 (2046)
29.	MWERU	*AFRICA*	5120 (1980)
30.	NETTILLING	*NORTH AMERICA*	5066 (1956)
31.	NIPIGON	*NORTH AMERICA*	4843 (1870)
32.	MANITOBA	*NORTH AMERICA*	4706 (1817)
33.	QINGHAI LAKE	*ASIA*	4489 (1733)

	LAKE	COUNTRY	SIZE in KM² (SQ MI)
34.	SAIMAA	*EUROPE*	4400 (1700)
35.	LAKE OF THE WOODS	*NORTH AMERICA*	4350 (1680)
36.	KHANKA	*ASIA*	4190 (1620)
37.	SARYGAMYSH	*ASIA*	3955 (1527)
38.	DUBAWNT	*NORTH AMERICA*	3833 (1480)
39.	VAN	*ASIA*	3755 (1450)
40.	PEIPUS	*EUROPE*	3555 (1373)
41.	UVS	*ASIA*	3350 (1290)
42.	POYANG	*ASIA*	3210 (1240)
43.	TANA	*AFRICA*	3200 (1230)
44.	AMADJUAK	*NORTH AMERICA*	3115 (1200)
45.	MELVILLE	*NORTH AMERICA*	3069 (1185)
46.	BANGWEULU	*AFRICA*	3000 (1200)

World's Longest Rivers

	RIVER	CONTINENT	LENGTH in KM (MILES)
1.	NILE	*AFRICA*	6650 (4132)
2.	AMAZON	*SOUTH AMERICA*	6400 (3976)
3.	YANGTZE (LONG RIVER)	*ASIA*	6300 (3917)
4.	MISSISSIPPI	*NORTH AMERICA*	6275 (3902)
5.	YENISEI	*ASIA*	5539 (3445)
6.	YELLOW RIVER (HUANG HE)	*ASIA*	5464 (3395)
7.	OB	*ASIA*	5410 (3364)
8.	RIO DE LA PLATA	*SOUTH AMERICA*	4880 (3030)
9.	CONGO (ZAIRE)	*AFRICA*	4700 (2922)
10.	AMUR (HEILONG JIANG)	*ASIA*	4444 (2763)
11.	LENA	*ASIA*	4400 (2736)
12.	MEKONG	*ASIA*	4350 (2705)
13.	MACKENZIE	*NORTH AMERICA*	4241 (2637)
14.	NIGER	*AFRICA*	4200 (2611)
15.	BRAHMAPUTRA	*ASIA*	3848 (2391)
16.	MURRAY	*AUSTRALIA & OCEANIA*	3672 (2282)

	RIVER	CONTINENT	LENGTH in KM (MILES)
17.	TOCANTINS	*ASIA*	3650 (2270)
18.	VOLGA	*EUROPE*	3645 (2266)
19.	INDUS	*ASIA*	3610 (2240)
20.	SHAAT AL-ARAB	*ASIA*	3596 (2236)
21.	MADEIRA	*SOUTH AMERICA*	3380 (2100)
22.	PURUS	*ASIA*	3211 (1995)
23.	YUKON	*NORTH AMERICA*	3185 (1980)
24.	SAO FRANCISCO	*SOUTH AMERICA*	3180 (1976)
25.	SYR DARYA	*ASIA*	3078 (1913)
26.	SALWEEN	*ASIA*	3060 (1901)
27.	SAINT LAWRENCE	*NORTH AMERICA*	3058 (1900)
28.	RIO GRANDE	*NORTH AMERICA*	3057 (1900)
29.	LOWER TUNGUSKA	*ASIA*	2989 (1857)
30.	DANUBE	*EUROPE*	2888 (1795)
31.	IRRAWADDY RIVER	*ASIA*	2727 (1694)
32.	ZAMBEZI	*AFRICA*	2693 (1673)
33.	VILYUY	*ASIA*	2650 (1647)

	RIVER	CONTINENT	LENGTH in KM (MILES)
34.	ARAGUAIA	*SOUTH AMERICA*	2627 (1632)
35.	GANGES	*ASIA*	2620 (1628)
36.	AMU DARYA	*ASIA*	2620 (1628)
37.	JAPURA	*SOUTH AMERICA*	2615 (1625)
38.	NELSON	*NORTH AMERICA*	2570 (1597)
39.	PARAGUAY	*SOUTH AMERICA*	2549 (1584)
40.	KOLYMA	*ASIA*	2513 (1562)
41.	PILCOMAYO	*SOUTH AMERICA*	2500 (1553)
42.	UPPER OB	*ASIA*	2490 (1547)
43.	ISHIM	*ASIA*	2450 (1522)
44.	URAL	*EUROPE*	2428 (1509)
45.	JURUA	*SOUTH AMERICA*	2410 (1498)
46.	ARKANSAS	*NORTH AMERICA*	2348 (1459)
47.	COLORADO	*NORTH AMERICA*	2333 (1450)
48.	OLENYOK	*ASIA*	2292 (1424)
49.	DNIEPER	*EUROPE*	2287 (1421)
50.	ALDAN	*ASIA*	2273 (1412)

World's Highest Mountains

	MOUNTAIN	COUNTRY	HEIGHT in Meters (Feet)
1.	MOUNT EVEREST	*NEPAL/CHINA*	8848 (29,029)
2.	K2	*PAKISTAN*	8611 (28,251)
3.	KANGCHENJUNGA	*NEPAL/INDIA*	8586 (28,169)
4.	LHOTSE	*NEPAL/CHINA*	8516 (27,940)
5.	MAKALU	*NEPAL/CHINA*	8485 (27,838)
6.	CHO OYU	*NEPAL/CHINA*	8188 (26,864)
7.	DHAULAGIRI I	*NEPAL*	8167 (26,795)
8.	MANASLU	*NEPAL*	8163 (26,781)
9.	NANGA PARBAT	*PAKISTAN*	8126 (26,660)
10.	ANNAPURNA I	*NEPAL*	8091 (26,545)
11.	GASHERBRUM I	*PAKISTAN/CHINA*	8080 (26,509)
12.	BROAD PEAK	*PAKISTAN/CHINA*	8051 (26,414)
13.	GASHERBRUM II	*PAKISTAN/CHINA*	8035 (26,362)
14.	SHISHAPANGMA	*CHINA*	8027 (26,335)
15.	GYACHUNG KANG	*NEPAL/CHINA*	7952 (26,089)
16.	ANNAPURNA II	*NEPAL*	7937 (26,040)

	MOUNTAIN	COUNTRY	HEIGHT in Meters (Feet)
17.	GASHERBRUM IV	*PAKISTAN*	7932 (26,024)
18.	HIMALCHULI	*NEPAL*	7893 (25,896)
19.	DISTAGHIL SAR	*PAKISTAN*	7884 (25,866)
20.	NGADI CHULI	*NEPAL*	7871 (25,823)
21.	KHUNYANG CHHISH	*NEPAL*	7823 (25,666)
22.	MASHERBRUM	*PAKISTAN*	7821 (25,659)
23.	NANDA DEVI	*INDIA*	7816 (25,643)
24.	CHOMO LONZO	*CHINA*	7804 (25,604)
25.	BATURA SAR	*PAKISTAN*	7795 (25,574)
26.	KANJUT SAR	*PAKISTAN*	7790 (25,558)
27.	RAKAPOSHI	*PAKISTAN*	7788 (25,551)
28.	NAMCHA BARWA	*CHINA*	7782 (25,531)
29.	KAMET	*INDIA*	7756 (25,546)
30.	DHAULAGIRI II	*NEPAL*	7751 (25,430)
31.	SALTORO KANGRI	*INDIA/PAKISTAN*	7742 (25,400)
32.	KUMBHAKARNA/ JANNU	*NEPAL*	7711 (25,299)
33.	TIRICH MIR	*PAKISTAN*	7708 (25,289)

	MOUNTAIN	COUNTRY	HEIGHT in Meters (Feet)
34.	GURLA MANDHATA	*CHINA*	7694 (25,171)
35.	SASER KANGRI I	*INDIA*	7672 (25,171)
36.	CHOGOLISA	*PAKISTAN*	7665 (25,148)
37.	KONGUR TAGH	*CHINA*	7649 (25,095)
38.	SHISPARE	*PAKISTAN*	7611 (24,970)
39.	TRIVOR	*PAKISTAN*	7577 (24,859)
40.	GANGKAR PUENSUM	*BHUTAN/CHINA*	7570 (24,836)
41.	GONGGA SHAN	*CHINA*	7556 (24,790)
42.	ANNAPURNA III	*NEPAL*	7555 (24,787)
43.	SKYANG KANGRI	*PAKISTAN/CHINA*	7545 (24,754)
44.	CHANGTSE	*CHINA*	7543 (24,747)
45.	KULA KANGRI	*BHUTAN/CHINA*	7538 (24,731)
46.	KONGUR TIUBE	*CHINA*	7530 (24,705)
47.	MAMOSTONG KANGRI	*INDIA*	7516 (24,659)
48.	SASER KANGRI II	*INDIA*	7513 (24,649)
49.	MUZTAGH ATA	*CHINA*	7509 (24,636)
50.	ISMOIL SOMONI PEAK	*TAJIKISTAN*	7495 (24,590)

Other Principal Mountains

	MOUNTAIN	COUNTRY	HEIGHT in Meters (Feet)
60.	JENGISH CHOKUSU	*KYRGYZSTAN/ CHINA*	7439 (24,406)
78.	JOMOLHARI	*BHUTAN/CHINA*	7326 (24,035)
	ACONCAGUA	*ARGENTINA*	6962 (22,840)
	OJOS DEL SALADO	*ARGENTINA*	6908 (22,664)
	TUPUNGATO	*ARGENTINA/ CHILE*	6801 (22,310)
	HUACARAN	*PERU*	6769 (22,205)
	TENGRI KHAN	*KYRGZYSTAN*	6695 (21,965)
	SAJAMA	*BOLIVIA*	6542 (21,463)
	CHIMBORAZO	*ECUADOR*	6310 (20,702)
	DENALI	*UNITED STATES*	6190 (20,310)
	LOGAN	*CANADA*	6051 (19,524)
	COTOPAXI	*ECUADOR*	5896 (19,344)
	KILIMANJARO	*TANZANIA*	5895 (19,340)
	CITLALTEPI	*MEXICO*	5699 (18,697)
	DEMAVEND	*IRAN*	5664 (18,582)
	ELBRUS	*RUSSIA*	5642 (18,510)

MOUNTAIN	COUNTRY	HEIGHT in Meters (Feet)
POPCCATEPETL	*MEXICO*	5453 (17,887)
LUCANIA	*CANADA*	5228 (17,150)
KENYA	*KENYA*	5200 (17,058)
ARARAT	*TURKEY*	5165 (16,945)
VINSON MASSIF	*ANTARCTICA*	4892 (16,050)
PUNCAK JAYA	*INDONESIA*	4884 (16.024)
MONT BLANC	*FRANCE*	4808 (15,774)
FAIRWEATHER	*UNITED STATES/ CANADA*	4670 (15,320)
RAS DASHEN	*ETHIOPIA*	4620 (15,158)
WEISSHORN	*SWITZERLAND*	4505 (14,780)
MATTERHORN	*SWITZERLAND/ ITALY*	4477 (14,690)
WHITNEY	*UNITED STATES*	4418 (14,495)
RAINIER	*UNITED STATES*	4392 (14,410)
LA PLATA	*UNITED STATES*	4371 (14,340)
COLIMA	*MEXICO*	4340 (14,236)
ELGON	*UGANDA/KENYA*	4321 (14,176)
GRAND COMBIN	*SWITZERLAND*	4314 (14,153)

MOUNTAIN	COUNTRY	HEIGHT in Meters (Feet)
PIKES PEAK	*UNITED STATES*	4301 (14,110)
FINSTERAAR-HORN	*SWITZERLAND*	4274 (14,022)
MAUNA KEA	*UNITED STATES*	4205 (13,796)
GANNET	*UNITED STATES*	4202 (13,785)
JUNGFRAU	*SWITZERLAND*	4158 (13,642)
CAMEROON	*CAMEROON*	4095 (13,435)
MONTE VISO	*ITALY*	3847 (12,621)
GROSSGLOCK-NER	*AUSTRIA*	3798 (12,463)
FUJI	*JAPAN*	3776 (12,388)
COOK	*NEW ZEALAND*	3753 (12,313)
TEIDE	*SPAIN*	3718 (12,198)
MAHAMERU	*INDONESIA*	3676 (12,060)
HOOD	*UNITED STATES*	3428 (11,245)
PICO DE ANETO	*SPAIN*	3404 (11,168)
ETNA	*ITALY*	3323 (10,902)
BAKER	*UNITED STATES*	3286 (10,778)
DEMPO	*INDONESIA*	3159 (10,364)

MOUNTAIN	COUNTRY	HEIGHT in Meters (Feet)
MONTCALM	*FRANCE*	3080 (10,105)
ST. HELENS	*UNITED STATES*	2950 (9677)
PULOG	*PHILIPPINES*	2934 (13,796)
RORAIMA	*BRAZIL/GUYANA/ VENEZUELA*	2810 (9219)
KATHERINE	*EGYPT*	2637 (8651)
DOI INTHANON	*THAILAND*	2594 (8510)
GALDHOPIGGEN	*NORWAY*	2469 (8100)
PARNASSUS	*GREECE*	2457 (8061)
OLYMPUS	*UNITED STATES*	2425 (7954)
KOSCIUZKO	*AUSTRALIA*	2230 (7316)
MITCHELL	*UNITED STATES*	2038 (6684)
WASHINGTON	*UNITED STATES*	1917 (12,060)
CIRQUE	*CANADA*	1573 (5160)
BEN NEVIS	*UNITED KINGDOM*	1345 (4413)
SNOWDON	*UNITED KINGDOM*	1085 (3560)
SCAFELL PIKE	*UNITED KINGDOM*	978 (3209)

World's Highest Waterfalls

	WATERFALL	CONTINENT	HEIGHT in Meters (Feet)
1.	ANGEL FALLS	*VENEZUELA*	979 (3212)
2.	TUGELA FALLS	*SOUTH AFRICA*	948 (3110)
3.	TRES HERMANAS FALLS	*PERU*	914 (2999)
4.	OLO'UPENA FALLS	*UNITED STATES*	900 (2953)
5.	YUMBILLA FALLS	*PERU*	896 (2940)
6.	VINNUFOSSEN	*NORWAY*	860 (2822)
7.	BALAIFOSSEN	*NORWAY*	850 (2789)
8.	PU'UKA'OKU FALLS	*UNITED STATES*	840 (2756)
9.	JAMES BRUCE FALLS	*CANADA*	840 (2756)
10.	BROWNE FALLS	*NEW ZEALAND*	836 (2743)
11.	STRUPENFOSSEN	*NORWAY*	820 (2690)
12.	RAMNELFJELLS-FOSSEN	*NORWAY*	818 (2684)
13.	WAIHILAU FALLS	*UNITED STATES*	792 (2598)
14.	COLONIAL CREEK FALLS	*UNITED STATES*	788 (2585)
15.	MONGEFOSSEN	*NORWAY*	773 (2536)
16.	GOCTA CATARACTS	*PERU*	771 (2530)

Other Principal Waterfalls

	WATERFALL	CONTINENT	HEIGHT in Meters (Feet)
17.	MUTARAZI FALLS	*ZIMBABWE*	762 (2500)
19.	JOHANNESBURG FALLS	*UNITED STATES*	751 (2464)
20.	YOSEMITE FALLS	*UNITED STATES*	739 (2425)
-	JIAO LUNG FALLS	*TAIWAN*	600 (2000)
-	RIBBON FALLS	*UNITED STATES*	491 (1612)
-	PISSING MARE FALLS	*CANADA*	350 (1150)
-	NOHKALIKAI FALLS	*INDIA*	340 (1115)
-	REICHENBACH FALLS	*SWITZERLAND*	250 (820)
-	BRIDALVEIL FALLS	*UNITED STATES*	189 (620)
-	VICTORIA FALLS	*ZAMBIA/ ZIMBABWE*	108 (355)
-	IGUAZU FALLS	*ARGENTINA/ BRAZIL*	82 (269)
-	HUANGGUOSHU FALLS	*CHINA*	78 (255)
-	NIAGARA FALLS	*UNITED STATES/ CANADA*	51 (167)
-	DETTIFOSS	*ICELAND*	44 (144)
-	RHINE FALLS	*SWITZERLAND*	23 (75)

World's Largest Cities

	CITY	COUNTRY	POPULATION
1.	TOKYO	*JAPAN*	38,140,000
2.	JAKARTA	*INDONESIA*	30,539,000
3.	CHONGQING	*CHINA*	30,484,000
4.	MANILA	*PHILIPPINES*	29,700,000
5.	DELHI	*INDIA*	29,000,000
6.	SEOUL	*SOUTH KOREA*	25,514,000
7.	MUMBAI	*INDIA*	24,400,000
8.	SHANGHAI	*CHINA*	24,183,000
9.	SAO PAULO	*BRAZIL*	21,735,000
10.	BEIJING	*CHINA*	21,707,000
11.	HO CHI MINH CITY	*VIETNAM*	21,310,000
12.	NEW YORK	*UNITED STATES*	21,045,000
13.	LAGOS	*NIGERIA*	21,000,000
14.	MEXICO CITY	*MEXICO*	20,893,000
15.	MUMBAI	*INDIA*	20,748,000
16.	GUANGZHOU	*CHINA*	20,130,000
17.	DHAKA	*BANGLADESH*	18,595,000
18.	OSAKA	*JAPAN*	17,150,000
19.	CAIRO	*EGYPT*	16,925,000
20.	KARACHI	*PAKISTAN*	16,900,000
21.	MOSCOW	*RUSSIA*	16,555,000
22.	BANGKOK	*THAILAND*	16,256,000
23.	CHENGDU	*CHINA*	16,045,000
24.	TIANJIN	*CHINA*	15,569,000
25.	LOS ANGELES	*UNITED STATES*	15,440,000

	CITY	COUNTRY	POPULATION
26.	KOLKATA	*INDIA*	15,215,000
27.	BUENOS AIRES	*ARGENTINA*	15,130,000
28.	TEHRAN	*IRAN*	14,630,000
29.	LONDON	*UNITED KINGDOM*	14,373,000
30.	XI'AN	*CHINA*	13,570,000
31.	LAHORE	*PAKISTAN*	13,569,000
32.	ISTANBUL	*TURKEY*	15,029,000
33.	SHENZHEN	*CHINA*	13,195,000
34.	KINSHASA	*DR CONGO*	12,960,000
35.	RIO DE JANEIRO	*BRAZIL*	12,644,000
36.	PARIS	*FRANCE*	12,245,000
37.	BAODING	*CHINA*	11,691,000
38.	LAHORE	*PAKISTAN*	11,545,000
39.	LIMA	*PERU*	11,460,000
40.	BANGALORE	*INDIA*	11,250,000
41.	HANOI	*VIETNAM*	10,955,000
42.	HARBIN	*CHINA*	10,929,000
43.	WUHAN	*CHINA*	10,892,000
44.	SHIJIAZHUANG	*CHINA*	10,879,000
45.	BOGOTA	*COLOMBIA*	10,705,000
46.	SUZHOU	*CHINA*	10,683,000
47.	LINYI	*CHINA*	10,563,000
48.	CHENNAI	*INDIA*	10,560,000
49.	NAGOYA	*JAPAN*	10,240,000
50.	NANYANG	*CHINA*	10,050,000

Other Principal Cities

CITY	COUNTRY	POPULATION
NAIROBI	*KENYA*	9,354,000
JOHANNESBURG	*SOUTH AFRICA*	9,335,000
CHICAGO	*UNITED STATES*	9,275,000
HONG KONG	*CHINA*	7,435,000
BOSTON	*UNITED STATES*	7,130,000
CASABLANCA	*MOROCCO*	6,862,000
MADRID	*SPAIN*	6,642,000
TORONTO	*CANADA*	6,630,000
BERLIN	*GERMANY*	6,144,000
SAN FRANCISCO	*UNITED STATES*	6,100,000
SINGAPORE	*SINGAPORE*	5,639,000
BARCELONA	*SPAIN*	5,475,000
ST. PETERSBURG	*RUSSIA*	5,351,000
SYDNEY	*AUSTRALIA*	5,120,000
MELBOURNE	*AUSTRALIA*	4,965,000
ADDIS ABABA	*ETHIOPIA*	4,568,000
ROME	*ITALY*	4,356,000
MILAN	*ITALY*	4,336,000
MONTREAL	*CANADA*	4,098,000
CAPE TOWN	*SOUTH AFRICA*	4,005,000
DUBAI	*U. ARAB EMIRATES*	4,000,000
ATHENS	*GREECE*	3,781,000
SAN DIEGO	*UNITED STATES*	3,318,000
BUDAPEST	*HUNGARY*	3,001,000
LISBON	*PORTUGAL*	2,827,000

CITY	COUNTRY	POPULATION
PRAGUE	CZECH REPUBLIC	2,678,000
AMSTERDAM	NETHERLANDS	2,411,000
VANCOUVER	*CANADA*	2,265,000
LAS VEGAS	UNITED STATES	2,227,000
HAVANA	*CUBA*	2,107,000
SAPPORO	JAPAN	1,970,000
AUCKLAND	NEW ZEALAND	1,643,000
JERUSALEM	*ISRAEL/PALESTINE*	1,254,000
NICE	FRANCE	1,006,000
NAPLES	ITALY	967,000
CANCUN	MEXICO	744,000
MIAMI	*UNITED STATES*	470,000
CAMBRIDGE	*UNITED KINGDOM*	280,000
VENICE	*ITALY*	260,000
DUBROVNIK	CROATIA	66,000

Printed in Poland
by Amazon Fulfillment
Poland Sp. z o.o., Wrocław

61403784R00066

TO

OLIVER

LOVE FROM

Oliver loves being under the sea. Whether it's exploring a sunken pirate ship, swimming with mighty whales or looking at big shells, he couldn't be happier.

But today was different. Oliver was about to meet the most majestic creature of the underwater world....

Oliver was gliding through the cool, clear water, hypnotised by the coral, when he heard something strange.

"Is that ... crying?" he said.

SOB! SOB! SOB!

Oliver swam towards the sound and stopped when he spotted an entrance to a deep, dark cave....

"I wonder what's in there?" Oliver thought as he drifted closer.

As he bobbed up and down a sea creature peeked out from the darkness!

"Err, he- hello?" he whispered.

Oliver could just about make out that he was pink with blue sticky-up hair. But he wasn't scary, he just looked very sad.

And he was carrying a gold crown.

The sea creature wasn't just any old sea creature – he was a king. But he might not be for much longer.

"I was having my afternoon snooze, and when I woke up the jewels from my crown were gone," he sniffled. "If I don't get them back, how can I be king?"

"Don't worry," said Oliver. "I'll help you find them. Whoever took them can't have gone far. Let's go!"

And so the search for the lost jewels began....

"There's one!" pointed Oliver.

"Oh no, the grumpy crabs have got it!" gasped the king.

SNAP! GRUMBLE, GRUMBLE! SNAP! SNAP!

Oliver quickly dodged round one, darted past another, ducked under a third and rescued the jewel from a snapping claw.

"I've got it!" he yelled.

"Quick, let's skedaddle," said the king. "They'll be grumpier than ever now!"

Up ahead, Oliver and the king saw a giant clamshell perched on a rock. Could a jewel be trapped inside?

"Hmm," said Oliver, "how do you get a clamshell to open up?"

"I don't know," said the king, "how do you get a clamshell to open up?"

"It's not a joke!" said Oliver, "but that gives me an idea...."

He grabbed a handful of seaweed and began to tickle.

HA HA HA! HA HA HA! HA HA HA!

The clamshell burst open and the king plucked out the jewel.

"Ta-dah, only two more left to find!" he cheered.

Suddenly, a dolphin whooshed past and darted upwards.

"Something fishy's going on," giggled Oliver, "let's go!"

They burst onto the surface where a pod of dolphins was jumping and spinning and diving.

SPLASH! SPLISH! SPLOSH!

And they were throwing around another jewel.

Oliver had to act fast. He threw his wallet up in the air to trick the dolphins. Then, he quickly caught the jewel.

"Three down, only one to go!" he smiled.

The only place left on the reef they hadn't searched was ...

THE SEAWEED FOREST!

"Are you s-s-sure you want to g-g-go in there?" stuttered the king nervously.

Oliver looked up at the towering hairy branches swaying back and forth. Big, spooky eyes blinked back at him from the darkness, but that didn't stop him.

"I'll be fine!" said Oliver as he flicked on his torch.

Oliver hadn't been in an underwater forest before, but it was fun.

As he swam upwards he suddenly came face-to-face with the cutest thing he'd ever seen – a gigantic octopus.

The octopus looked startled and darted off. And as he did, eagle-eyed Oliver spotted the last jewel.

"Come back!" he shouted.

But the octopus disappeared.

Oliver needed a plan.

He kicked his flippers harder and harder and swam faster and faster through the seaweed to get ahead of the octopus.

Then he stopped, hid and kept very still.

It wasn't long before the seaweed started to rustle. He waited for just the right moment, and then....

"BOOOO!" yelled Oliver.

"AHHHHHHHH!" wailed the octopus.

Oliver quickly jumped out and rescued the final jewel.

Oliver carefully pressed the jewels into the king's crown and swam up to place it on his head.

"Ready?" asked Oliver.

"Ready!" smiled the king.

As Oliver lowered the crown all the fishy friends let out a big cheer, and all around them looked like awesome fireworks.

WOO-HOO! HOORAY!

"Oliver, you're my hero!" declared the king.

"I can't thank you enough," said the king. "If there's anything I can do for you, just name it."

"Well, there is one small thing," smiled Oliver. "Can you please let the jewel thieves out? They were only playing."

"Consider it done," said the king, "I guess they've learned their lesson now."

And with that, Oliver turned, waved goodbye and began to swim home, daydreaming of his next BIG adventure....

TIME OUT

MEET SANTA?
Maybe I'll...

EXPLORE SPACE?

HELP A DINOSAUR?

Oliver, look out for more **Mini Adventures** books.
Go to www.orangutanbooks.co.uk

Story by Jane Kent
Illustrated by Jo Lindley
Designed by Jane Gollner

orangutan

First published by Orangutan Books in 2019
Hometown World Ltd, 1 Queen Street, Bath BA1 1HE

Visit
www.orangutanbooks.co.uk
Follow us @orangutanbooks

ISBN 978-1-78979-490-8

Printed in Italy
HTW_PO201907

MIX
Paper from responsible sources
FSC® C023419
FSC
www.fsc.org